MICHAEL JORDAN

MICHAEL JORDAN

LIFE LESSONS
FROM HIS AIRNESS

DAVID H. LEWIS

CASTLE POINT BOOKS
NEW YORK

For Mom, Dad, Sis, Bella,

and the loves of my life, Ezra and Sebastian.

With assists from David A., Helaine, and Aimee.

—D.H.L.

www.castlepointbooks.com

The Castle Point Books trademark is owned by Castle Point Publishing, LLC. Castle Point books are published and distributed by St. Martin's Publishing Group.

ISBN 978-1-250-28159-3 (paper over board)
ISBN 978-1-250-28160-9 (ebook)

Design by Katie Jennings Campbell
Composition by Noora Cox
Illustrations by Gilang Bogy

Our books may be purchased in bulk for promotional, educational, or business use. Please contact your local bookseller or the Macmillan Corporate and Premium Sales Department at 1-800-221-7945, extension 5442, or by email at MacmillanSpecialMarkets@macmillan.com.

First Edition: 2022

10 9 8 7 6 5 4

"NEVER SAY NEVER, BECAUSE LIMITS, LIKE FEAR, ARE OFTEN JUST AN ILLUSION."

CONTENTS

On the court, he was an unstoppable force. His scoring average of 30.1 points per game eclipsed every player before him and all who have followed. He'd leap so high off the ground on a dunk that he'd hit his head on the rim. He set NBA records like it was just another day at the office. When it came to basketball, no one in the world compared to him. Michael Jeffrey Jordan (a.k.a. MJ, the GOAT, Air Jordan, Mike, His Airness) is one of the most talented and beloved athletes of our time.

STAT ⚡ Over the course of his career, Michael Jordan racked up 165 40-point games, 32 50-point games, and 5 60-point games.

He was an offensive assassin who could also dominate on defense, leading the league in steals over three different seasons and earning the Defensive Player of the Year award in 1988. He was chosen as MVP All-Star three times.

Off the court, his celebrity power and business acumen has dictated style trends and sold more product over time than anyone thought possible, from the perennially popular Nike Air Jordan sneakers to the baggy shorts players still wear today (Michael wanted enough room under his Chicago Bulls shorts to wear his University of North Carolina shorts) to the "Be Like Mike" slogan that earned Gatorade decades of brand recognition. He was one of the first athletes to star in commercials and reap sky-high profits. Today he still makes billions of dollars in endorsement deals, far more than any of his contemporaries.

Even though Michael was almost superhuman as a player, he was and is as human as the rest of us, and that's what makes his story so intriguing. We watched as he broke down in tears after finally winning his first title. We witnessed him struggling through the sudden death of his father. He wrestled with life-altering decisions, struggled to know when to retire, and bravely took a hiatus to try his hand at baseball. He was held to a higher standard and was asked to defend his every mistake, including his bold career choices, combative style, and penchant for gambling. He has been criticized and praised in the same breath repeatedly but managed to prevail as a leader and an icon.

While other players might have suffered from their mistakes, he used every failure as inspiration to push himself harder. He lost to the

Detroit Pistons—he used that frustration to break their winning streak. He fell short of winning a championship for years—he went on to win six of them. He lacked a consistent jump shot—he developed an unstoppable turnaround fadeaway jump shot. He turned disappointment into self-improvement:

> *"I've missed more than 9,000 shots in my career. I've lost almost 300 games. Twenty-six times I've been trusted to take the game-winning shot and missed. I've failed over and over and over again in my life. And that is why I succeed."*

He's nothing if not complicated.
Teammates and competitors have called him selfish, maniacal, and ruthless. His obsession with winning at all costs rubbed people the wrong way. His blistering trash talk was infamous. He spurned criticism during his basketball career and guarded his legacy with a passion. But these are the same character traits that made him a winner.

Maybe we can't jump four feet off the ground.
Or catch so much air that we can put our head six inches above a basketball rim. And there's no way we could score 32,292 points in the NBA. But we can learn what it takes to become a leader and a champion from the man who did all those things and more. We can learn from Michael's approach to the game, his tireless work ethic, and his handling of coaches and teammates.

So why will we be talking about Michael Jordan for decades and centuries to come?
Because what he did on the court was otherworldly. What he showed us was inspiring. What he teaches us is timeless.

His jaw-dropping dunks, clutch shooting, and fierce determination will live on forever. When you are that good of a competitor, that memorable a player, that much of a trendsetter, you never disappear. You carry on as a legend, and your life becomes a valuable collection of lessons learned.

STAY FIERCE

CHAPTER 1

There's nothing ordinary about Michael Jordan, a man who was born to play basketball. His burning desire to win was always clear from the look on his face: eyes steely, tongue out. He'd lick his lips right before torching an opponent on the court. When you look back at his childhood and early years, you see the origins of Michael's passion for leadership and his burning desire to outdo everyone else.

DEVELOP A HEALTHY RIVALRY

Michael was born in Brooklyn, New York, arguably the mecca of basketball, on February 17, 1963. The young Jordan didn't have much time to adjust to his humble surroundings or soak in the city's basketball culture because, by age two, his family had already left for a new life in Wilmington, North Carolina. His father, James, and his mother, Deloris, felt the streets of Brooklyn were too dangerous for their family. They wanted a safer environment for their kids.

Michael was the fourth of five children in the family: two older brothers (James Jr. and Larry), an older sister (Deloris), and a younger sister (Roslyn). His brother Larry, older by just 11 months, had the most significant influence on his life—and game. Michael gives credit to his brother for instilling a winning mentality in him from a very early age:

> *"When you come to blows with someone you absolutely love, that's igniting every fire within you. And I always felt I was fighting Larry for my father's attention. . . . So my determination got even greater to be as good if not better than my brother."*

Michael's older brother never made it to the NBA, but he had talent and a drive that would rub off on his little brother. Larry is five feet eight inches tall, much shorter than his brother, but he could leap 44 inches into the air—nearly as high as his famous sibling at the height of his game. Larry pushed his little brother and knew early on that Michael was destined to be something special. "His level of play was just so much higher than the rest of us," Larry said. "People ask me all the time if it bothered me, but I can honestly say no because I had the opportunity to see him grow. I knew how hard he worked."

HARNESS YOUR FRUSTRATIONS

Michael was a bit of a combative child, and in middle school, that kind of behavior got him suspended. Michael's mom, Deloris, was deeply invested in keeping her son from getting into trouble. She worked hard to keep him in line. By the time he got to high school, his grades had improved considerably. He was always good in sports—excelling in basketball, football, and baseball—but going into high school, he dreamed of making the varsity basketball team. And when Michael was focused on something, even at this early age, nothing stood in his way.

Michael stood out in baseball from the start. He was an outstanding center fielder and pitcher who threw

"SOMETIMES A WINNER IS JUST A DREAMER WHO NEVER GAVE UP."

DRAWN TO DANGER

One day, a young Michael and his brothers decided that it would be fun to dance in the mud inside a pigpen and make snorting noises. One pig became agitated and chased Mike (as he was known as a kid) toward an electric fence. As he leaped over the fence to safety, he caught his leg and tripped, sending an electric shock surging through his body and burning his chest.

You would think Mike would've learned about the dangers of rural life, but no. Later on, he decided to try his hand at chopping wood. Unfortunately, he misjudged where the ax would land and cut his big toe, after which he ran screaming to his parents. To this day, he is missing an inch of his big toe.

---

45 consecutive shutout innings for Laney High School. He was less confident on the basketball court. Part of that had to do with his height. During his sophomore year, the older, more experienced players called Mike "Peanut" and "Shagnut." He took the abuse but was determined to develop his skills to make them pay for the slight.

As a sophomore trying out for the varsity team, he was under six feet tall and couldn't dunk. That was a problem. Michael knew he needed to grow in order to dominate in basketball. His father tried to comfort him: "You have it in your heart," he'd say. "The tallness is within you. You can be as tall as you want to be in your thinking."

When Michael finally tried out for the team in 1978, it didn't go well. He didn't make the varsity squad, and this left him feeling disrespected by his high school coach. He was placed on a list of players for the JV team. He cried in his room after seeing the list. To make matters worse, one of his close friends, Leroy Smith, who was a sophomore and stood close to six feet seven inches tall, had made the varsity team, so he knew it was possible. He took it as a statement that he wasn't good enough. And then he took it as a personal challenge.

"TO WIN,
YOU HAVE TO LOSE.
TO BE SUCCESSFUL,
YOU'VE GOT TO
HAVE SOMETHING
THAT'S NOT
SUCCESSFUL.
TO BE HAPPY,
YOU HAVE TO HAVE
DISAPPOINTMENT."

"When I got cut from the varsity team as a sophomore in high school, I learned something," Michael said. "I knew I never wanted to feel that bad again. I never wanted to have that taste in my mouth, that hole in my stomach."

According to his coach, the real story was that sophomores rarely start on the varsity team, plus Mike Jordan was only five feet ten at the time, so his height was an added disadvantage. Michael allowed himself a little time, then used the episode as rocket fuel to launch his career. He brought up the "varsity cutting" episode almost 30 years later in his Hall of Fame speech:

> *"When he made the team and I didn't, I wanted to prove not just to Leroy Smith, not just to myself, but to the coach who actually picked Leroy over me, I wanted to make sure you understood—you made a mistake, dude."*

His teacher remembered Michael's fierce determination: "He never wanted to lose in anything," said Ruby Smith, a physical education teacher at Laney. "That was inborn into him. I normally get to school between 7 and 7:30. Michael would be at school before I would. Every time I'd come in and open these doors, I'd hear the basketball. Fall, wintertime, summertime. Most mornings I had to run Michael out of the gym."

Michael grew four inches in his junior year, became a starter on the varsity team, and never looked back. This was when his work ethic became legendary. He worked out all the time and quickly became the alpha dog on the Laney High School basketball team, averaging more than 20 points per game. He was assertive now, not shy.

The experience of getting cut stayed with Michael for the rest of his basketball career. "Whenever I was working out and got tired and figured I ought to stop, I'd close my eyes and see that varsity list in the locker room without my name on it," he explained. "That usually got me going again." Michael was adept at taking a negative and turning it into a positive, even using perceived failures or slights to motivate himself and push himself to do great things.

NEVER BE SATISFIED

Michael never let himself rest on his acheivements. If he scored 20, he thought it should have been 30. If he scored 30, it should have been 40. Then, if he hit the game-winning shot, he would dwell on a bad pass he had made rather than simply celebrate the shot.

In his senior year of high school, Michael averaged an unheard-of triple-double, with double digits in scoring, assists, and rebounds. Michael elected to play in the McDonald's All American Games, a prestigious honor for any high schooler, scoring 30 points and grabbing the MVP trophy. He was on everyone's list for stardom. Even though he loved baseball and was good at it, basketball was his true calling. He took his talents to the University of North Carolina at Chapel Hill.

LIFE LESSONS FROM HIS AIRNESS

- HAVE FAITH IN YOURSELF.
- FAILURE COMES BEFORE SUCCESS.
- HARD WORK PAYS OFF.
- USE ADVERSITY FOR MOTIVATION.
- NEVER SETTLE FOR LESS.

"IF YOU PUSH ME TOWARD SOMETHING THAT YOU THINK IS A WEAKNESS, THEN I WILL TURN THAT PERCEIVED WEAKNESS INTO A STRENGTH."

BECOME A LEADER

CHAPTER 2

A young Michael Jordan was challenged to become a leader right out of high school. It may seem like he had always been a leader, but back when Michael was a skinny kid from Wilmington, North Carolina, he was known more for his jaw-dropping dunks and aerial forays around the rim than his commanding role on a basketball team.

When he arrived at Chapel Hill to play for the University of North Carolina, he was the low man on the totem pole as a freshman. Talented? Yes. But conventional wisdom said he had to find his place and avoid stepping on too many toes, especially the more senior players. Rarely did his coach, Dean Smith, play freshmen. Finding his place in college basketball and being the new guy on the team was an uphill battle Michael hadn't yet fought.

"I WAS YOUNG, BUT I HAD NO TIME TO BE NERVOUS."

Michael relished a challenge and loved proving people wrong, so he pushed himself by setting ambitious goals in his early college career. UNC was loaded with talented players, including future Hall of Famer James Worthy. Instead of deferring to Worthy, however, Michael created a challenge that would fuel his freshman career. He told himself that he would be the best player on the team by the end of the year.

"He wanted to learn, and he wanted to grow quickly," Worthy said about Michael the freshman. "From month to month, from game to game, he was soaking up information. Once he got something and added it to the raw talent that he already had, it was really explosive to see."

TO BECOME A LEADER, YOU MUST FOLLOW A LEADER

Michael looked up to his college coach, Dean Smith. He listened and learned under his tutelage. From a very young age, Michael knew that he was talented, but he needed to work on teamwork, discipline, and the fundamentals of the game. Coach Smith was a disciplinarian with a huge heart. He knew when to wrap an arm around a player and when to dole out tough love.

Michael loved to be pushed by Smith, whose focus on discipline was music to Michael's ears. In a published letter from 1983, coach Smith wrote to the young player, assigning him eight ways to improve his game. He wrote that Michael's

HAVE A PLAN B

Michael Jordan had a backup plan if his professional basketball career did not work out. He wanted to be a meteorologist to pursue his interest in the weather and geography, which explains why he majored in cultural geography.

development of these skills would make him a better basketball player and (more importantly) would help the team accomplish great things.

As good as Michael was as an individual, he needed to learn to be part of a winning team. Dean Smith was the only man capable of putting limits on Michael's explosive game; he kept him below 20 points scored per game on average (a benchmark for any great scorer) for all three seasons of his college career, thus making sure the "I" stayed out of "team." It would take a strong coach like Smith to help Michael learn to value the team's success over his own.

THE RIGHT SIDE OF HISTORY

Coach Smith's influence went beyond the basketball court. He set an example as a good human being. Coach Smith had shown great courage in 1967 by taking a stand against segregation. He recruited and gave a scholarship to UNC's first African American basketball player, Charlie Scott, who played his first game on December 2, 1967. Michael was moved by this 15 years later when he came to play for Smith.

He saw the man that coach Smith was and how the teams he led became better than the sum of their parts. Michael said shortly after Dean Smith's death in 2015:

"He was more than a coach—he was my mentor, my teacher, my second father. Coach was always there for me whenever I needed him, and I loved him for it. In teaching me the game of basketball, he taught me about life."

HARD WORK PAYS OFF

Michael's tireless work ethic was second to none, and it never waned. He was hard on people, but never harder than he was on himself. His attention to detail was what separated him from other "hardworking" players. He was known for pushing exhausted teammates back onto the floor after a two-and-a-half-hour practice to go one-on-one. He was always trying to get better and modeled that behavior for others. He never cheated the game or wasted his talents.

A HABIT WORTH KEEPING

As his professional career advanced, Michael's workouts continued to reflect his tireless work ethic. His longtime trainer, Tim Grover, would tell anyone who'd listen about how dedicated Michael was to his training, which was most evident when Michael was shooting the film *Space Jam*.

Grover outlined Michael's movie set regiment this way: "A typical day on the set would entail about 40 minutes of conditioning. This included stretching, running, and various basketball drills. Then he'd go to the movie set. At lunchtime, he'd work out with weights for about an hour and a half. Then he'd be back on set from 3 p.m. to 7 p.m. From 7:30 p.m. to about 10 p.m., he'd play basketball."

Michael was all about keeping the competition going, especially in training. The conventional way of doing things wasn't going to cut it. While playing for the Chicago Bulls, he made sure that practice came first. He created an early-morning training session called Breakfast Club.

"THERE IS NO 'I' IN TEAM, BUT THERE IS IN WIN."

"MY WHOLE LIFE HAD ALWAYS BEEN ABOUT BEING THE BEST BASKETBALL PLAYER I COULD BE."

"FAILURE ALWAYS MADE ME TRY HARDER NEXT TIME."

"It was like having a gathering every single morning of individuals for the purpose of getting them on the same page, getting them prepared," Grover said. "You know a lot of guys now start thinking about the game when they get to the arena. With Breakfast Club, when we were working out at 5 a.m., 6 a.m., or 7 a.m., that's when our preparation started."

RISE TO THE TOP

By the end of his freshman year at UNC, Michael had aged like a fine wine. His maturity went beyond his years, and he became a lead scorer and a pivotal part of the team, an unprecedented achievement for a first-year player. He led the UNC Tar Heels to an NCAA title in 1982. North Carolina was trailing 62–61 in the title game with 32 seconds remaining. Although Michael was only a freshman, he was chosen to take the last shot on a team filled with experienced and talented leaders like James Worthy, Sam Perkins, and Matt Doherty. Michael was passed the ball and stepped into a jump shot, burying the basket with 17 seconds to go, sealing UNC's fate.

Air Jordan was born during that winning moment:

> *"It was destiny. Ever since I made that shot. Everything has just fallen into place for me. If that shot hadn't gone in, I don't think I would be where I am today."*

Michael played two more years at UNC before entering the NBA draft in 1984. His game had improved so much that many thought he'd be selected No. 1 overall in the draft, a badge of honor for any player. It surprised those who knew his potential when he was selected third. Michael used that perceived

"IF YOU RUN
INTO A WALL,
DON'T TURN AROUND
AND GIVE UP.
FIGURE OUT
HOW TO CLIMB IT,
GO THROUGH IT, OR
WORK AROUND IT."

slight, being drafted behind Sam Bowie, a lesser player who was chosen second, as fuel to prove people wrong. It was a constant theme throughout his life, taking a negative and turning it into a positive.

When he arrived in Chicago to start his rookie year with the Bulls, he had to prove himself all over again. Rookies were not treated well, no matter how much fanfare they brought with them. Yet, Michael never deviated from who he was at his core. He would work harder and push himself further than anyone else—and ultimately become a leader. He was fearless:

> *"Whoever is the team leader . . . , I'm going to be going after him. And I'm not going to do it with my voice. Because I had no voice. I had no status. I had to do it with the way that I played."*

REBOUND FROM SETBACKS

As Michael Jordan's game and presence progressed, so did the resentment from other more established players. His resolve was tested, along with his intestinal fortitude and belief in himself. But he never wavered.

During the All-Star game in his rookie year, some players allegedly decided to freeze out Michael. As a result, he had limited touches on the ball, and his playing suffered. In the end, he scored only seven points. But Michael would not let the story end there.

In the game following the All-Star game, he managed to score 49 points, grab 15 rebounds, dish out five assists, and collect four steals. He always had an answer for the critics.

ONE ROAD TO SUCCESS

Michael's first season in the NBA was so successful that he was named Rookie of the Year; his stats were so good they looked like video game stats. Of course, anyone would have been thrilled and satisfied with that kind of year, but not Michael. He knew that winning was the only thing that mattered, and the Bulls

STAT ⚡ Michael Jordan averaged 28.2 points, 6.5 rebounds, 5.9 assists, and 2.4 steals in 82 games during his rookie year with the Chicago Bulls.

hadn't been winning as much as they should have.

In Michael's first season playing for the Bulls, the team lost more games than they won and were bounced out of the playoffs in the first round.

Michael took the pain of losing and resolved to learn from it. Because, as he already knew from experience, "the best comes from the worst."

LIFE LESSONS FROM HIS AIRNESS

- ● DON'T SETTLE FOR BEING GOOD. AIM TO BE GREAT.
- ● EMULATE A LEADER WHO INSPIRES YOU.
- ● NEVER LET YOUR EGO GET IN THE WAY OF SUCCESS.
- ● NOTHING CAN REPLACE HARD WORK.
- ● LEAD BY EXAMPLE, AND OTHERS WILL FOLLOW.

"IF YOU'VE
GOT SUCCESS
IN YOUR HOUSE,
YOU FIND A WAY TO
MANAGE SO THAT
EVERYBODY PROSPERS
AND EVERYBODY
IS VIEWED
AS CHAMPIONS."

MAKE GREATNESS YOUR BRAND

CHAPTER 3

We watch our icons closely. We scrutinize how they walk, how they dress, how they carry themselves. The more they're in the public eye, the more we try to copy them. In a Nike ad, Charles Barkley, responding to the same kind of pressure that Michael felt, declared, "I'm not a role model." He was pushing back on the trend of young kids emulating their sports heroes and reminding fans that athletes are flawed human beings just like everyone else. But the fans bought into the role-model ideal whether the athlete wanted it or not, especially when it came to Michael Jordan. He was on the scene, and everyone wanted to look, act, play, and sound like Mike. Maybe even name their kid after him.

BREAK THE RULES

Michael lived a charmed life in college. After winning the NCAA championship, he had everyone's attention. Even at this early age, he didn't entirely trust all the fame or attention. He was careful to make sure he didn't say the wrong things. He sensed he was becoming a role model but was reluctant about being pushed into the limelight too fast. He was aware of his developing image and protected it.

When he got drafted into the NBA by the Chicago Bulls in 1984, Michael exploded onto the scene with a charismatic edge that was hard to look away from. With his pinstripe suit, tightly cropped hair, and sleek tie, he looked like a sinewy six-foot-six-inch superhero. He held up his No. 23 Bulls uniform to a vast New York City audience and set his career in motion. Everyone heralded his arrival, most notably Nike, a company known more for its running shoes than its basketball shoes. However, that would change the minute the company signed the young Michael to a basketball shoe deal in his rookie season. The Nike Air Jordan line of sneakers was born soon after.

Michael was heavily involved in designing the Nike Air Jordan 1. Everyone loved the black and red hues of the prototype that he wore in several games. The NBA, however, was quick to warn him that the Air Jordan I violated their shoe color guidelines. Nike later aired a television commercial that added fuel to the fire and glamorized this act of rebellion: "On September 15, Nike created a revolutionary new basketball shoe. On October 18, the NBA threw them out of the league."

A SHOE TO BUILD A DREAM ON

The original Nike Air Jordan 1 "Bred" sneaker was released in 1985 in black and red leather with a white midsole—and with a shocking-at-the-time sticker price of $64.99.

"DREAMS ARE REALIZED BY EFFORT, DETERMINATION, PASSION, AND STAYING CONNECTED TO THAT SENSE OF WHO YOU ARE."

"YOU HAVE TO EXPECT GREAT THINGS OF YOURSELF BEFORE YOU CAN DO THEM."

Michael continued to wear his cutting-edge Air Jordans while Nike paid the extraordinary $5,000 fine per game. No other player had pushed the limits for a shoe or been so successful at selling one. It was the first sign that Michael had become part of the mainstream fashion conversation and was expertly building his brand.

During Michael's first NBA All-Star game in February 1985, he defiantly wore the banned sneakers and two gold chains (which were also against regulations during the regular season) to the Slam Dunk Contest. Even though Michael didn't win that year's contest, his unreal athleticism paired with his new flashy line of shoes streaking across the court on TV screens around the world made him bigger than Nike ever could have imagined.

He would go on to win back-to-back Slam Dunk Contests in 1987 and 1988. His signature take-off-from-the-foul-line dunk in 1987 has been viewed on YouTube more than 12 million times (and counting), with his Air Jordans helping him land a perfect slam dunk score of 50. Nike and Michael were taking off and soaring to new heights.

SHOW THEM WHO YOU ARE

After its release, the Air Jordan line of sneakers became the most popular shoe in the world. With the help of Nike, Michael created the Jordan Brand, his signature line. It expanded beyond shoes to encompass ready-to-wear and leisure attire. Throughout the 1980s and 1990s, Air Jordans enjoyed the spotlight in countless music videos on the feet of rappers and singers. They were donned by sports figures and CEOs alike. Anyone alive during

EXCEED EXPECTATIONS

The Air Jordan 1 sneaker, which Nike anticipated would bring in a projected $3 million, reportedly earned the brand $126 million.

that time was aware of the street cred you earned if you had a pair of those shoes. "For a kid, it was almost like owning a lightsaber from *Star Wars*," rapper Nas said. "You needed that shoe to be like him. It was more than a status symbol—you knew that this guy was the guy."

Wearing a pair of Jordans made people of all ages feel as though they had the power to take flight and be like Mike. In Nike's famous ad, the saying, "It's gotta be the shoes," became a motto for how unfathomably good Michael was. The ad shows Mars Blackmon, a Spike Lee character, asking Mike what makes him great:

> *Spike Lee: Yo, Mars Blackmon here with my main man Michael Jordan. Yo Mike, what makes you the best player in the universe? Is it the vicious dunks?*

Michael Jordan: No, Mars.

SL: Is it the haircut?

MJ: No, Mars.

SL: Is it the shoes?

MJ: No, Mars.

SL: Is it the extra-long shorts?

MJ: No, Mars.

SL: It's the shoes, right?

MJ: No, Mars.

Michael knew that to grow his brand and connect with fans, he needed to take himself less seriously and even to poke fun at himself. His skill in selling this image led to further success. He set lasting style trends

DECADES OF FAME AND STYLE

Air Jordans have remained popular to this day, with more than twenty-five versions designed and debuted. People of all ages still line up outside sneaker stores to get their hands on the latest edition of the sneaker.

"IF I HAD A CHANCE TO DO IT ALL OVER AGAIN, I WOULD NEVER WANT TO BE CONSIDERED A ROLE MODEL. IT'S LIKE A GAME THAT'S STACKED AGAINST ME."

that extended beyond shoes, like the shaved head, baggy shorts, and ankle-high socks that remain in vogue today. But the real Michael knew that his game and his endless determination were the actual value he brought. He laid that truth bare in a follow-up Nike commercial:

"It's not about the shoes. It's about knowing where you're going. Not forgetting where you started. It's about having the courage to fail. Not breaking when you're broken. Taking everything you've been given and making something better. . . . It's about being who you were born to be."

YOU CAN'T PLEASE EVERYONE

There was, eventually, a price to pay for this notoriety as a trendsetter. The Air Jordans became so popular and were so expensive that stories emerged of them being stolen right off kids' feet. Michael took a lot of heat for this, even though it was Nike's decision to sell them at such a high price. He was also drawn into the debate over how much the shoe factory workers in Asia were getting paid—or not getting paid—to make his shoes.

Michael took some other hits regarding his public image. He was criticized for not being an advocate for African Americans and not being engaged enough with politics. Some wanted him to be a stronger voice when it came to the social and political issues of the day. But that wasn't Michael:

"I wasn't a politician when I was playing my sport. I was focused on my craft. Was that selfish? Probably. But that was my energy. That's where my energy was."

He had opinions, but he didn't have Muhammad Ali's outspokenness or the activist instincts of Bill Russell or Kareem Abdul-Jabbar. Instead, he got involved with charity work as a way to help others and pay it forward.

The long list of charities that have benefited from Michael's generosity over the past few decades includes the Boys & Girls Clubs of America, the Jackie Robinson Foundation, and the United Negro College Fund, to name a few. He put his money where his heart was. Perhaps his most notable contribution was when he donated his 2001–02 NBA salary to 9/11 charities.

STAT ⚡ **Over five years, Michael Jordan donated more than $30 million to the National Museum of African American History and Culture, the Make-A-Wish Foundation, hurricane relief funds, and Chicago-area charities.**

"I NEVER THOUGHT
OF MYSELF AS
AN ACTIVIST.
I THOUGHT OF
MYSELF AS A
BASKETBALL PLAYER."

STILL GOT IT

Michael earns more money from endorsement deals today (more than $3 billion) than any NBA player has earned from their salary and endorsements combined.

After he retired from basketball, Michael gradually grew into the role of activist and found additional causes that mattered to him.

In an appearance on *The Today Show*, he explained why he was inspired to give so much away:

> *"I feel a certain warmth about it. If I feel like I'm making a difference, that's all that matters to me. . . . At the end of the day, if you know you're providing services for people in need, that's all that matters."*

KNOW HOW TO SELL IT

Michael liked to entertain his fans. His gregarious, intoxicating smile was a true asset for advertisers—he was the perfect pitchman. Whether it was for Gatorade, Hanes, McDonald's, or Wheaties, he played to his audience, and his fans ate it up. His power to add value to every product he touched was known as "the Jordan Effect."

The NBA knew what he brought to their coffers. He boosted gate receipts, television revenue, and viewership. He helped sell apparel and led the way for other players to do the same. His value grew exponentially. Even with so many people expecting and demanding his selling power, Michael kept his cool and managed his endorsement deals with acumen.

> *"In college, I never realized the opportunities available to a pro athlete. I've been given the chance to meet all kinds of people, to travel and expand my financial capabilities, to get ideas and learn about life, to create a world apart from basketball."*

GO OUTSIDE YOUR COMFORT ZONE

Michael's brand reached unthinkable heights in 1996. He'd been in the public consciousness for a decade and a half on a level never before achieved by an athlete. What else could Michael do? Well, he could be the star of a live-action animated movie. The movie *Space Jam*, where Michael stars alongside a medley of beloved Looney Tunes characters, made a big splash in the mid-1990s and performed well at the box office, earning more than $200 million worldwide. It played well to both basketball and non-basketball audiences. It was never more evident Michael's celebrity power went beyond sports.

LIFE LESSONS FROM HIS AIRNESS

- **BREAK THE RULES; MAKE A STATEMENT.**
- **BUILD YOUR BRAND.**
- **DON'T TRY TO BE SOMEONE YOU'RE NOT.**
- **KNOW YOUR WORTH.**
- **TAKE A CHANCE ON SOMETHING BIG.**

"EVERY TIME I
STEPPED ON THE FLOOR
I REPRESENTED
MY FAMILY,
THE CHICAGO BULLS,
THE NBA,
BECAUSE MY DESIRE
WAS STRONG."

TRUST IN
HARD WORK

CHAPTER 4

Michael Jordan pushed himself so hard that he started winning individual awards the moment he got into the NBA. He won the Rookie of the Year award (1985), the Defensive Player of the Year award (1988), and the NBA All-Star Game MVP trophy (1988). In 1986, he made the NBA All-Defensive Team (1986). He even won a scoring title with one of the highest averages ever recorded—37.1 points per game (1987).

But his signature moment came in 1988 when he faced off against Dominique Wilkins, a fellow high-flyer, nicknamed "the Human Highlight Film." In the final round of that year's Slam Dunk Contest, Michael took off from the other end of the court to the foul line, where he launched himself forward, floated in the air—tongue out, legs splayed—and slammed the ball into the basket. This signature spread-eagle move would become an enduring logo for the Jordan brand. Michael received a perfect score of 50 from the judges for this incredible take-off-from-the-foul-line dunk. Even though the Slam Dunk contest was an exhibition, Michael took it as seriously as he took every game. In the end, it paid off.

At this point, Michael had won almost every award an individual player could imagine. In the early part of his basketball career, being selfish had helped him gain success. But those individual achievements weren't enough for this uber-competitive man. He knew he would be judged on championships and didn't want his legacy to be that of a selfish player. He was ready to work toward a new goal, one that required him to rely on and reach out to others.

"Once you get to your highest level, then you have to be unselfish. Stay reachable. Stay in touch. Don't isolate."

KNOW WHAT YOU'RE WORKING FOR

Michael's quest to win a championship was part of his

"YOU HAVE COMPETITION EVERY DAY BECAUSE YOU SET SUCH HIGH STANDARDS FOR YOURSELF THAT YOU HAVE TO GO OUT EVERY DAY AND LIVE UP TO THAT."

persistent quest to be the greatest. When Michael came into the league, the Boston Celtics' Larry Bird and the Los Angeles Lakers' Magic Johnson were the gold standards. They were winning multiple championships, sometimes battling each other directly for them. Michael wanted what they had. He had won the NCAA title, so he had a taste of what it felt like to win something that big. But he was ready for more. Unfortunately, the team roster wasn't championship caliber just yet. In his first three years in the league, the Bulls made it to the playoffs but couldn't make it past the first round.

There were plenty of other great players in the league in the same situation as Michael who'd been playing their hearts out and winning a ton of awards, yet hadn't managed to win an NBA championship. Charles Barkley, Patrick Ewing, Karl Malone, John Stockton, and many others—all players on the list of the NBA's 50 Greatest Players of all time—were fairly or unfairly considered flawed because they hadn't won a title. In contrast, Larry and Magic were thought of as the true "winners."

Dirk Nowitzki, who won a title after 12 seasons in the league, described how he handled the years leading up to that accomplishment: "For me, I was prepared to live with the fact that I wasn't going to win a title. One of my big idols is Charles Barkley. And I never have looked at him lesser because he didn't win a championship." But that kind of acceptance wasn't anywhere to be found in Michael Jordan. He would not stop working until he had reached the highest level and gained the most prestige.

While a championship eluded him in his early years on the Bulls, the spotlight did not. Michael enjoyed plenty of signature moments during the playoff games. One of those moments occurred in a game against the Cleveland Cavaliers in 1989, when he made what is referred to as "the Shot." Craig Ehlo, a defender, was hanging all over Michael. Cleveland was up 100–99 with three seconds left. At the last second, Michael made a jump shot over Ehlo from the foul line to win the series and send the Bulls to the next round of the 1989 playoffs.

"IF YOU
DO THE WORK,
YOU GET REWARDED.
THERE ARE
NO SHORTCUTS
IN LIFE."

Michael couldn't contain his emotions. He pumped his fists in the air after the shot and ran all over the court. His teammates mobbed him. In the end, he didn't win the championship, but it had been so close that he could almost touch it.

The following year, he elevated his performance yet again. He scored a career-best 69 points versus the Cavs in a 117–113 overtime win. He hit 23 of 37 field goals, went 21-for-23 on free throws, and grabbed 18 rebounds. "It was my best game ever, by far," he said afterward, "especially because we won." But he was one man and he needed more help to go further. As good as Michael was, he couldn't carry the entire team on his shoulders. Something had to change.

EVERYONE NEEDS HELP

Michael liked playing for Chicago Bulls coach Doug Collins, and they had some success. But it wasn't until Phil Jackson came on board that Michael excelled as a teammate as well as a player.

Jackson brought a calmer, more collaborative approach to the team.

He had won a championship with the New York Knicks as a player. Jackson believed in using a triangle offense, which Michael didn't buy into at first because it took the ball out of his hands. With Collins, Michael always had the ball, and he loved that. But that approach had yielded no championships and in some ways, it made the team more vulnerable. So at the beginning of Jackson's coaching tenure, he explained the thinking behind the triangle offense to Michael. He told Michael why he didn't want him to dominate possession: "The spotlight is on the ball. If you're the guy that's always going to have the ball, teams can generate a defense against that."

While it took time to master this new approach, Michael soon discovered how effective the triangle could be once players learned to read and react to the defense. *Spacing* between the players was key. The basic structure of the offense consisted of the "sideline triangle" on one side of the floor and a two-man game on the weak side (where the ball wasn't). Eventually, Michael flourished in the

"TALENT WINS GAMES, BUT TEAMWORK AND INTELLIGENCE WINS CHAMPIONSHIPS."

triangle, and it became a valuable tool for the Bulls. (Jackson would later take this offense to the Lakers as the head coach and guide Kobe Bryant to his five titles.)

Even with this new offensive style and a stellar coach, Michael still needed help. He needed better players around him. The 1987 NBA draft of Scottie Pippen changed everything. The strapping, defensive genius was just what Michael needed. Pippen was Robin to Jordan's Batman. They shared a special bond. Pippen had been the missing piece, and Michael knew it.

Pippen explained their strong connection:

"We grew up together and we defended each other. That respect we had on the court, that competitiveness we took through to the top—it was special. That was the respect we had for each other because we had to be on the court to do what we did. We had to be dominant."

Now Michael had all the pieces in place for a serious run at a championship. But there was a formidable barrier blocking him from getting it: the Detroit Pistons.

> STAT ⚡ Michael is the only guard to earn 2,500-plus points in five straight seasons, doing so in a spell from 1986–1991 and barely missing out by double-digit points in 1991–92 before another year of 2,500-plus points in 1992–93.

STAY STRONG THROUGH ADVERSITY

The Detroit Pistons, a.k.a. "the Bad Boys," were a collection of hard-nosed players who played the game on the edge. Some people called them dirty for their tactics, while others considered them a throwback team that played its game below the rim. Michael liked to play his game above the rim. Something had to give.

Michael had beaten the Pistons in the regular season with individual efforts that defied logic. He scored 59 points in a Bulls win on Easter Sunday. The year before, he scored 61 points in an overtime victory. But the Pistons knew they had to put their defensive clamps down on Michael in the playoffs. "The Jordan Rules" were born when the Pistons employed a rough-and-tumble targeted plan to keep Michael under wraps.

Chuck Daly, the Pistons' coach who helped develop "The Jordan Rules," outlined the protocol to keep Jordan from scoring:

"If Michael was at the point, we forced him left and doubled him. If he was on the left wing, we went immediately to a double team from the top. If he was on the right wing, we went to a slow double team. He could hurt you equally from either wing—hell, he could hurt you from the hot-dog stand—but we just wanted to vary the look. And if he was on the box, we doubled with a big guy. The other rule was, any time he went by you, you had to nail him. If he was coming off a screen, nail him. We didn't want to be dirty—I know some people thought we were—but we had to make contact and be very physical."

The Bulls-Pistons rivalry was one of the greatest of all time. Michael Jordan and the Pistons' Isaiah Thomas went at it on and off the court. Michael never hid his disdain for Thomas, who has always defended the hard-boiled approach the Pistons had to take. "We knew [Jordan] was the greatest player," Thomas said. "We had to do everything from a physical standpoint to stop him."

The Bulls and Pistons played each other in the Eastern Conference twice and once in the semifinals. For two straight years, the Pistons beat the Bulls to reach the NBA finals. The Pistons won back-to-back championships during that period.

There were hard fouls, violent fouls, and—overall—no love lost between the two sides throughout their battles. Michael was bruised and battered after each losing series, thanks to the "The Jordan Rules." Yet, despite his physical fatigue, he stayed unflappable. He knew only one way to be: strong and determined. Every summer after he lost to the Pistons, he worked even harder.

In 1991, Michael faced the Pistons for the third straight time in the conference finals and finally broke through. In a heated series, the Bulls swept the Pistons 4-0. Detroit's behavior at the end of game 4 stirred up controversy: The Pistons walked off the court with time left on the clock and refused to shake the Bulls' hands, a customary gesture at the end of a series. This behavior went against everything Michael believed. Despite his hypercompetitive nature, he had always tried to do the right thing and show good sportsmanship. He played hard but fair. He shook the hands of the Pistons after every series he lost to them. This slight didn't sit well with him.

PERSEVERANCE PAYS OFF

Michael had finally gotten over the hump of beating the Pistons. Now he had to find enough energy to play in the finals against the Magic Johnson–led Los Angeles Lakers.

Michael played a masterful series. His strength and determination were on full display. His talent was

"PEOPLE DIDN'T
BELIEVE ME
WHEN I TOLD THEM
I PRACTICED HARDER
THAN I PLAYED,
BUT IT WAS TRUE."

A LIST OF LEGENDS

In 1999, Michael Jordan topped ESPN's list of the Greatest North American Athletes of the 20th Century. He beat out Babe Ruth, who was ranked second. He was also ranked above the beloved Muhammad Ali and Kobe Bryant.

never more striking than when he leaped to great heights, switched hands in midair, and kissed the ball off the backboard. His body seemed to defy physics, floating for an impossible amount of time. The Bulls won the series in five games. Michael won the series MVP, but he knew he couldn't have done it without Pippen.

"I didn't win without Scottie Pippen, and that's why I consider him my best teammate of all time," Michael would later gush. "He helped me so much in the way I approached the game, in the way I played the game. Whenever they speak 'Michael Jordan,' they should speak 'Scottie Pippen.'"

One of the lasting images of the postgame celebration is of Michael crying in the locker room with the championship trophy in his hands.

His father, James, was right by his side. The joy he felt sharing that win with his father was evident. His dad's pride was also apparent. Suddenly, fans could see Michael's soft side. His love of the game was laid bare. The relief of winning a championship was so evident in his face. The monkey was off his back. He was now a champion.

SET GOALS AND CRUSH THEM

Michael understood the importance of not letting up. He knew he couldn't rest on his laurels. So he came back more determined than ever to win back-to-back championships in the 1991–92 season. Many players had won championships, but few had won back-to-back titles. Up to this point, only three other teams had won multiple titles in a row; Michael wanted the Bulls to be the fourth on that list.

"I'M ALL ABOUT CHALLENGES AND SEEING IF I CAN GO OUT AND SEE IF I CAN ACHIEVE SOMETHING.

Michael relished a challenge. He liked to create a tension that would drive him toward excellence. The loftier the challenge, the more motivated he was.

The Bulls had an impressive 67–15 record in the regular season. They got through all three playoff round series in the Eastern Conference, including a very physical seven-game series against the New York Knicks. Then they faced the Portland Trail Blazers in the NBA Finals, where Michael was pitted against Clyde "the Glide" Drexler—two of the top shooting guards in the league. Many people felt that Drexler was the closest player to Jordan in terms of talent; they were also close statistically. Michael averaged 30.1 points, 6.4 rebounds, and 6.1 assists in the regular season, and had won the MVP award. Drexler averaged 25.0 points, 6.6 boards, and 6.7 assists per game. Portland battled the Bulls to a six-game series, with the Bulls and Michael prevailing.

STAT ⚡ Famous for coming up big in clutch moments, Michael only fell short of 20 points six times in 179 playoff games.

"WHEN I LOSE THE
SENSE OF MOTIVATION
AND THE SENSE TO
PROVE SOMETHING AS
A BASKETBALL PLAYER,
IT'S TIME FOR ME
TO MOVE AWAY
FROM THE GAME
OF BASKETBALL."

"EVERYBODY HAS TALENT, BUT ABILITY TAKES HARD WORK."

Michael being Michael, he had been offended by all the comparisons with Drexler. By the end of the series, much to his satisfaction, nobody was comparing the two. Drexler averaged close to 25 points for the series, while Michael averaged close to 36 (and scored a whopping 46 points in game 5).

Michael knew that he'd need to chase another goal to stay engaged and perform at his best.

So he set his sights on a three-peat. Only two franchises, the Boston Celtics and the Los Angeles Lakers, had won three or more championships in a row.

Michael was ready for the Bulls to join those elite teams. He fixed his sights on the 1992–93 season and pinpointed the goal of winning a third championship. With laser focus, he was determined to carry out his plan.

LIFE LESSONS FROM HIS AIRNESS

- SET CHALLENGES FOR YOURSELF AND DO WHATEVER IT TAKES TO ACHIEVE THEM.
- BELIEVE IN THE PROCESS AND STICK TO IT WITH A PASSION.
- GIVE CREDIT WHERE CREDIT IS DUE.
- ANYTHING IS POSSIBLE IF YOU DECIDE IT IS.

DEMONSTRATE GRACE UNDER PRESSURE

After Michael and the Bulls won their second title, they celebrated in the streets of Chicago with a parade, where Bulls center Will Perdue said to the gathered fans, "The first time was neat. The second time was one heck of a feat. This time I had one hell of a seat. The third time will be oh-so-sweet."

Everyone on the team had that three-peat in the back of their mind as a goal to pursue, but they were also ready to enjoy their summer vacation and rest their weary bones from the grind of playing 10 months a year for the past two seasons. There would be no rest for Michael and his teammate Scottie Pippen, however. They were heading to Barcelona to play in the Olympics that summer. It was a big deal. The United States was sending the "Dream Team" of NBA players (plus one college player) to Spain to bring home the gold.

Four years earlier, the U.S. had failed to win the gold, taking home the bronze. The pressure was on the 1992 U.S. Olympic squad, but it mainly rested on the shoulders of the greatest player on the planet. And he was tired. At that point, Michael had been playing for 21 straight months. Not even Michael could be expected to perform at a high level for that long. But he was going to try.

The U.S. Olympic "Dream Team" was led by Michael, but included many Hall of Fame players, such as Charles Barkley, Larry Bird, Magic Johnson, and John Stockton. The rest of the world didn't know what hit them.

"The 'Dream Team' blew it wide open," Michael said about his fame. He hit a new level of worldwide stardom.

"I think that was when I couldn't go anywhere in the world and walk the streets. I used to go to Paris or Milan and just walk the streets, and no one would know. I could sit outside with my family and friends and just enjoy. But ever since the 'Dream Team,' things have just totally gone berserk. No matter where I go in Europe, it's no different than the States."

Michael understood that Magic and Larry were in the twilight of their careers, so he assumed leadership. The "Dream Team" dominated, and Michael put on his famous display of high-flying dunks for the fans to see. The world-class team won every game by at least 30 points, making it look easy to take home the gold.

With very little rest, Michael shifted his focus from the Olympics to prepare for the NBA season. "We knew the season was going to be a grind," said Phil Jackson before the start of it. "No matter what approach we were taking, [going for a third title] was going to wear us down mentally and physically. We just did the best we could and took each day as its own."

DROWN OUT THE HATERS
Michael was, and still is, a self-proclaimed competition junkie.

"NOTHING OF VALUE COMES WITHOUT BEING EARNED."

He bets exorbitantly on golf, cards, and other games that catch his interest. He had plenty of money in the 1990s, but he never bet on NBA games, so there was nothing illegal about it. Regardless, his propensity for gambling didn't sit well with those who wanted a squeaky-clean role model. The criticism went from a whisper to a roar when he gambled in Atlantic City before a playoff game in 1993. He had to defend his behavior in interviews where he defined his gambling as a hobby rather than a habit. "I can stop gambling," Michael asserted in a 1993 interview with Connie Chung. When she asked if he had a gambling problem, he replied, "I have a competition problem, a competitive problem."

Michael took the criticism lightly. He didn't enjoy the negative attention, but he knew to keep it in perspective. As if to show the critics how little their opinion mattered, he continued to gamble whenever he wanted and is still a betting man to this day:

> *"My job was to go out there and play the game of basketball as best I can. People may not agree with that. I can't live with what everyone's impression of what I should or what I shouldn't do."*

GET TO WORK

Michael knew he could not afford to be distracted by the drama surrounding his gambling. So he channeled all of his energy into his biggest quest to date: winning three consecutive NBA titles with the

---

STAT ⚡ **During the 1992 Summer Olympics, Michael set an Olympic men's record with eight steals in the opening game against Angola. Then he repeated this same feat of athleticism the next day against Croatia.**

"I PLAY TO WIN, WHETHER DURING PRACTICE OR A REAL GAME."

Chicago Bulls. This would prove to be his highest mountain to climb.

He would have to sustain excellence on the court, stay motivated no matter how tired he felt, and be the kind of leader his team needed, all while fielding questions from the hungry press. Fortunately, the more stress Michael was under, the better he performed.

Michael would spend the whole 1992–93 season grinding, pushing, and excelling despite being mentally and physically exhausted. He had several nagging injuries, but he could deal with those. During regular-season games, the Bulls played well, finishing second behind the New York Knicks in the Eastern Conference. Michael knew, however, that the playoffs were the real test of a team. By the time the Bulls reached the playoff season, they were ready to go.

Michael came under intense scrutiny in the playoff series against the Knicks. The Bulls lost the opening two games of the series, with Michael hitting only 22 of 59 shots. Some attributed his lackluster performance to his late-night jaunt to Atlantic City before game 2. However, others thought the Knicks' roughhouse tactics were more likely a contributor.

The Bulls looked to be in trouble, but Michael would not be denied.

Instead, he took his me-against-the-world attitude and used it as motivation. In a pivotal game 5 at Madison Square Garden, Michael taught everyone who doubted him a lesson, getting a triple-double of 29 points, 14 assists, and 10 rebounds. As a result, Michael and the Bulls won their third straight title, beating the Phoenix Suns in six games.

You could see it on his face. It was Michael's most challenging year, despite how spectacularly it ended. But he never wavered. He embraced the pressure. He used the tension and challenges to build himself up when most people would crumble. He dug as deep as he had to until he discovered in himself a deep well of inner strength.

SHOW DIGNITY IN THE WAKE OF TRAGEDY

Michael was at the peak of his career. He had just won his third straight NBA title after winning a gold medal at the 1992 Olympics with the "Dream Team." But in the summer of 1993, Michael's life would come crashing down around him.

After being reported missing for several weeks, James Jordan, Michael's father, was found dead, his body abandoned in a creek. According to reports, he had been sleeping in his car on the side of the road when two men approached the vehicle. They planned to rob him, but instead, he was shot dead.

Michael's relationship with his father was well documented. He leaned heavily on his dad and always sought

STAT ⚡ Michael won his seventh scoring title in 1992–93. He shot nearly 50 percent from the field that season and 83.7 percent from the line. In addition, he snagged 6.7 rebounds, stole 2.8 balls per game, and had an average of 5.5 assists per night.

> **STAT ⚡ Michael scored 40 or more points in four consecutive NBA Finals games in 1993, setting a record. He finished with an NBA Finals record of 41.0 points per game.**

his guidance. So his father's sudden, brutal passing left a massive hole in Michael's life. What hurt Michael even more was public speculation that the incident might be related to Michael's gambling, something Michael vehemently denied. He could have easily lashed out, but he kept his composure with the media and his critics. "I am trying to deal with the overwhelming feelings of loss and grief in a way that would make my dad proud," Michael said a few days after his father's death. Still, he was clearly hurt by the attacks on his character:

> *"I simply cannot comprehend how others could intentionally pour salt in my open wound by insinuating that faults and mistakes in my life are in some way connected to my father's death."*

Michael was fortunate to have the strength of his mother, Deloris, to lean on. She told Michael to be thankful for what he had and for the time he had with his father. As the months went by, he reflected on how his dad lived his life and how he would have wanted Michael to go on with his:

> *"One of the things that [my dad] always taught me is that you have to take a negative and turn it into a positive, so I started looking to the other side of it, and that helped me get through it."*

LISTEN TO YOUR GUT

One of the things that made Michael such an incredible player and competitor was that he followed his instincts. He knew when to push and when to pull back. In 1993, he determined that it was time to pull back. After winning three titles, Michael wanted to retire from basketball.

In a shocking announcement in October 1993, he revealed his decision to the world. Sure, he was only 30, but he had put a lot of miles on his body. Without his father there by his side, he knew that playing basketball would be different on a profoundly emotional level. So, at a press conference, he did his best to explain his mindset.

"THE GOOD PART ABOUT BEING FAMOUS IS BEING ABLE TO HELP PEOPLE. THE HARD PART IS EVERY DAY YOU HAVE TO BE IN A GOOD MOOD BECAUSE THAT IS WHAT PEOPLE EXPECT. YOU LEARN TO GET GOOD AT IT."

"[My father's death] made me realize how short life is, how quickly things can end, how innocently. And I thought that there are times in one's life when you have to put games aside. I wanted to give more time to my family. I've been very selfish about centering things on my basketball career. Now it's time to be unselfish with them."

TAKE BIG RISKS

As fans came to grips with Michael leaving basketball, he settled into his new life. He played golf regularly and spent time with his family. But he wasn't content for long. His competitive juices were still flowing, and they needed an outlet.

In one of his last conversations with his dad, they had debated whether baseball was still on the table as a worthy pursuit for Michael. James Jordan had played semipro baseball and raised his son to love the sport. Michael had played baseball up until his senior year of high school. He recalled confiding in his dad that we was thinking about retiring from basketball to play baseball, and his dad was overwhelmingly supportive. "Do it, do it," Michael remembers him saying. He'd always loved watching his son play.

In 1994, he decided to honor his dad's wish and try his hand at professional baseball. His brother Larry was not surprised when he got word of this decision: "[Michael] always loved playing baseball. We thought we were going to be Major League Baseball players, me and him growing up as kids."

Michael felt a sense of freedom once he'd made the decision. He felt closer to his father for having made it. But a lot of fans and media critics didn't get it. They thought that playing baseball would tarnish his basketball legacy.

It wasn't really in Michael's personality to care what others thought. He did what made him happy, and playing baseball was going to make him happy. And he had no intention of failing. So he took this bold career move very seriously.

"MY FATHER USED TO SAY THAT IT'S NEVER TOO LATE TO DO ANYTHING YOU WANTED TO DO. AND HE SAID YOU NEVER KNOW WHAT YOU CAN ACCOMPLISH UNTIL YOU TRY."

PLAY BALL

Some people thought Michael's transition to baseball was a stunt. To Michael, it was an opportunity. He signed on to play for the Birmingham Barons, the Double-A affiliate of the Chicago White Sox, on February 7, 1994. He went into this new venture with characteristic dedication, a solid work ethic, and an unrivaled commitment to playing a completely different game from the one that had made him a star. In general, baseball demands fast-twitch muscles and incredible hand-eye coordination. It also requires a little more bulk and strength than basketball, where constant movement, muscle contractions, and explosive bursts of speed and

"I CAN ACCEPT FAILURE; EVERYONE FAILS AT SOMETHING. BUT I CAN'T ACCEPT NOT TRYING."

power are key. It was difficult to imagine how a single person could encompass all of these qualities.

Michael wound up batting .202 for the 1994 season. Not great, but he did drive in 51 runs and steal 30 bases. It was, however, fated to be a short-lived experiment in athleticism. When the players went out on strike rather than give in to the baseball owners' demands for a salary cap, Michael made the difficult decision to give up baseball. The strike lasted 232 days. Michael couldn't stall his burgeoning baseball career that long, especially when he needed to learn so much so quickly.

Many felt that Michael would have made it to the Major Leagues if he had stuck with baseball. Others weren't convinced. Michael didn't care either way. He had done what he came to do: fulfill his dream and honor his late father.

DON'T DENY YOUR TRUE LOVE

Michael was away from basketball for 21 months. He was ready to go home. On March 18, 1995, he shook the basketball world once again with a two-word press release: "I'm back."

The next day, he suited up for the Bulls, wearing his new number, 45. (His signature number 23 had been retired.) He showed very little rust, scoring 19 points, grabbing six rebounds, and dishing out six assists against the Indiana Pacers in his first game back.

He accomplished the impossible against the New York Knicks four games later, showing everyone that he hadn't lost his edge. He scored 55 points in what was later called the "Double Nickel game" and added one more to the many signature Michael Jordan moments in his career.

There was one last change that Michael needed to make to feel like he was truly back. During a second-round playoff game against the Orlando Magic, Michael committed a turnover that led to the Magic's game-winning fast-break dunk. The player that stripped the ball, Nick Anderson, took a jab at him after the game: "No. 45 doesn't explode as No. 23 used to. No. 45 is not No. 23. I couldn't have done that to No. 23."

After that game, Michael got rid of jersey No. 45. He switched back to No. 23 in game 2 and scored 38 points, leading the Bulls to a win. But, unfortunately, Michael and the Bulls would eventually lose that series. He wouldn't get another title that year, but he had assured everyone that No. 23 was back for more.

LIFE LESSONS FROM HIS AIRNESS

- WHEN THE GOING GETS TOUGH, TRY EVEN HARDER.
- TAP INTO YOUR INNER STRENGTH DURING THE MOST TROUBLING OF TIMES.
- CHALLENGE YOURSELF AND SEIZE NEW OPPORTUNITIES.
- DO WHAT YOU LOVE, NO MATTER WHAT IT IS.

"IF YOU ARE
CONFIDENT
YOU HAVE DONE
EVERYTHING
POSSIBLE TO
PREPARE YOURSELF,
THEN THERE IS
NOTHING TO FEAR."

ONCE A CHAMPION, ALWAYS A CHAMPION

CHAPTER 6

When Michael sets his mind to do something, he gets it done.
Win multiple championships? Check. Play baseball? Check. Play basketball again? Check. He was always readying himself and his body for the next goal. When Michael played baseball, he reshaped his body to handle the rigors of the game. Then, when he returned to basketball two years later, he understood that he was older and had to recondition his body once again.

He had been skinny in high school and college. He'd gained lean muscle at the beginning of his pro basketball career, then added some bulk to withstand the punishment he was getting from teams like the Detroit Pistons and the New York Knicks. For baseball, he worked with a trainer to add even more muscle weight in the right areas while strengthening his core and toughening up his hands. Before he returned to playing basketball, he did the work needed to shape his body into a combination of strength, flexibility, muscle, and guile—this was Jordan 2.0.

COME BACK STRONGER

At the start of the 1995–96 season, Michael looked fresh. Back in his role as the leader of the Bulls, he demanded excellence and commanded commitment. He had built up the power in his body to win, and he was ready for the challenge of proving his critics wrong. They said Michael couldn't return to basketball and be the player he once was. He knew that if he slacked off or got lazy, the season could go sideways.

"THE MINUTE YOU GET AWAY FROM FUNDAMENTALS— WHETHER IT'S PROPER TECHNIQUE, WORK ETHIC, OR MENTAL PREPARATION— THE BOTTOM CAN FALL OUT OF YOUR GAME, YOUR SCHOOLWORK, YOUR JOB, WHATEVER YOU'RE DOING."

But playing baseball had only deepened his competitive hunger:

"What baseball provided was the energy of camaraderie, to see guys go out and do things they have love in their hearts for, even though they're not getting paid a lot. That rejuvenated me as an athlete."

He would focus that newfound energy on silencing the doubters and winning another championship.

The Bulls added a player by the name of Dennis Rodman. Rodman was a free-spirited player who had won two championships with the "Bad Boy" Pistons, the team that had been a thorn in Michael's side for so long. Now one of those thorns was on his team.

Rodman was markedly different from Michael, but MJ respected how hard he worked. During the 1995–96 regular season, the Bulls with Rodman played the game with such precision, vigor, and cohesiveness that they lost only three times in their first 44 games. With a 41–3 record, they were on pace to become the best regular-season team in the history of the NBA, a stat that renewed Michael's energy and revved him up for even greater success.

Michael never set out to break records. They just happened along the way to a greater goal. When Michael got close to the record, he zeroed in on the goal with laser focus. The Bulls would finish the regular season with a 72–10 record, the best regular season in NBA history (an achievement that the Golden State Warriors eventually beat in the 2015–16 season):

"[Getting the best record in NBA history] was not a goal. It was not something we started out the season trying to achieve. But when it got within reach, we wanted to do it. Don't forget, we didn't start out the season saying we were going to win 70 games. We started out the season saying we're going to win a championship."

His concentration hit a new level. He took home the regular-season MVP award, but that didn't surprise

"IT'S HEAVY-DUTY TO TRY TO DO EVERYTHING AND PLEASE EVERYBODY."

anyone. What did surprise others was that, at 33 years old, he was better than ever.

Even though Michael had dedicated the season to silencing his remaining critics and using any perceived slight to keep himself motivated, deep down, he knew the critics would never go away. However, he also knew that he could drown them out and get the job done. As Michael said to a reporter after his 70th win, "I came into this season with a lot to prove... That's the motivation right now."

The Bulls were just as dominant in the playoffs as they were in the regular season. They beat the Miami Heat (3–0), the Knicks (4–1), and the Orlando Magic (4–0). Michael and the Bulls made it look easy.

They went on to play the Seattle SuperSonics in the championship. The SuperSonics put up a fight, but it wasn't enough. The Bulls won 4–2. Michael had won his fourth championship and first postbaseball retirement title. But, more importantly, he'd won his first championship since his father had passed away.

Michael was captured on live television in the postgame locker room, lying on the floor clutching

the trophy. The emotions of the moment got to him. He was crying uncontrollably, expressing the mixed feelings of joy at having won and grief in being unable to share the win with his father.

MOTIVATION COMES FROM WITHIN

While others might have been satisfied with four titles, Michael Jordan was still motivated to achieve more. The prospect of winning back-to-back titles again was driving him forward. He knew that the more titles he won, the more incomparable and legendary he'd become. He loved that he was already being heralded as one of the greatest of all time. Now he wanted to be *the* greatest of all time. But he knew that he couldn't do it alone and that the team's success would have to come before his:

"There are plenty of teams in every sport that have great players and never win titles. Most of the time, those players aren't willing to sacrifice for the greater good of the team. The funny thing is, in the end, their unwillingness to sacrifice only makes [their] individual goals more difficult to achieve."

The following year, Michael, Scottie Pippen, and Dennis Rodman set out together with one common goal: Repeat the 1995–96 season. Again, they breezed through the regular season with a 69–13 record, coming oh so close to breaking their own record. They pushed their way through each round of the playoffs and arrived at the finals playing against the Utah Jazz, led by Karl Malone and John Stockton. The two were masters of the pick and roll—a

STAT ⚡ In 1996–97, Michael led the league for the ninth time in scoring with 29.6 points per game along with 5.9 rebounds, 4.3 assists, and 1.71 steals per game. Michael was voted to the All-NBA First Team and the All-Defensive First Team.

"ONE THING I BELIEVE
TO THE FULLEST
IS THAT IF YOU
THINK AND ACHIEVE
AS A TEAM, THE
INDIVIDUAL ACCOLADES
WILL TAKE CARE
OF THEMSELVES."

"WHAT IS LOVE?
LOVE IS PLAYING
EVERY GAME AS IF
IT'S YOUR LAST!"

basic play that was hard to defend even when everyone saw it coming.

Malone had never won a championship, so he was extra hungry. He had just beaten out Michael that year for the MVP award, but that only helped to motivate Michael and his team to come out on top.

In game 1 of the finals, Michael hit a buzzer-beating jump shot. But the Jazz, with the roar of their fans as loud as a jumbo jet engine, continued to be a formidable foe in the games that followed. The series was tied 2–2. Then, in the fifth game of the finals, Michael showed up not feeling like himself. He was sick and dehydrated, but ready to play his heart out anyway. He scored 38 points in 44 grueling minutes, including the game-winning 3-pointer with 25 seconds remaining.

After the game, Michael was even more exhausted than usual. "I almost played myself into passing out," he admitted. The game became known as the "Flu Game," but Michael determined later on that it was a delivery pizza he ate that caused his sickness. "So, it really wasn't the flu game," Michael clarified. "It was food poisoning."

Nonetheless, Michael's performance was incredible considering how weak he'd felt all night. But he wasn't done yet. He helped the Bulls win game 6 to take the title. Then, for the fifth time in five finals, he took the MVP award home with him. He now had a ring for each finger:

> *"I've always believed that if you put in the work, the results will come. I don't do things half-heartedly. Because I know if I do, then I can expect half-hearted results."*

Maybe he had a ring for each finger, but nothing was going to stop him from working toward outfitting the fingers on his other hand.

PREPARATION FUELS SUCCESS

Michel has what some call God-given talent, but he is also one of the hardest-working athletes of all time. The blood, sweat, and tears he poured into each game are legendary. In basketball, players in their mid-30s tend to wind down and play more minor roles. They come off the bench occasionally. Play fewer minutes. Not Michael; he played better than ever in his 30s. And he was not a bit player. He was definitely still primetime.

In 1998, when Michael was 36, the Bulls were going for their second three-peat. The playoffs were a bit of a test as the Bulls ran into Reggie Miller and the Indiana Pacers. Indiana played a rugged style of basketball, but Michael had seen that before. The Bulls won in seven games and advanced to a rematch with the Utah Jazz. It proved to be a tough series, but in game 6, with the Bulls leading 3–2 in Utah, Michael added a shining new moment to his highlight reel.

First, he hit a jumper with about 41 seconds left to cut the Jazz's lead to one. Then he stole the ball from Malone and raced to the other end of the court. He held the ball outside the 3-point line, dribbled, and then executed one of the most memorable moves in NBA finals history. With ten seconds on the clock, Michael dribbled one way, crossed over the other way (some people say he pushed off on his defender Bryon Russell), and then pulled up and made a jumper with just over five seconds remaining to make the game-winning and series-clinching shot.

Michael earned the title of finals MVP (his sixth) again after scoring 45 points in that series-winning game. Six rings and counting.

CAN'T STOP; WON'T STOP

On January 13, 1999, Michael retired again. He was burnt out and had lost his drive. He was a perfectionist, so if he couldn't play at the highest level, he didn't want to play at all anymore. When asked if he would ever come back, Michael said he was "99.9 percent" sure he would not. It was clear this was one of the hardest decisions he'd ever made.

"CHAMPIONS DO NOT BECOME CHAMPIONS WHEN THEY WIN AN EVENT, BUT IN THE HOURS, WEEKS, AND MONTHS, AND YEARS THEY SPEND PREPARING FOR IT."

In his retirement speech, he told a room full of reporters not to worry about him. He assured them that he would devote himself to the challenges of raising kids:

> *"People say, 'Well Michael Jordan doesn't have any challenges away from the game of basketball.' I dispute that. Being a parent is very challenging. If you have kids you know that and I welcome that challenge. I look forward to it. I will live vicariously through my kids if they play the game of basketball or if they don't. . . . I look forward to that."*

About a year later, the retired superstar found something else to channel his competitive energy. On January 19, 2000, he bought an ownership stake in the Washington Wizards. As a minority owner and president of basketball operations, he was excited to announce his return to the NBA. No one knew whether he would play again, but they suspected he might when he hired his former Bulls coach, Doug Collins, to coach the Wizards and started training. He was 38 years old when he stepped back onto the court as a Wizard after a three-year absence.

Michael knew he didn't have a lot of seasons left in him, but he missed the game and wanted to teach younger players all he'd learned in his career:

> *"I am returning as a player to the game I love because during the last year and a half, as a member of Washington Wizards' management, I enjoyed working with our players, and sharing my own experiences as a player. I feel there is no better way of teaching young players than to be on the court with them as a fellow player, not just in practice, but in actual NBA games."*

He took his role as a mentor seriously from day one. "My challenge when I came back," he explained, "was to face the young talent, to dissect their games, and show them maybe that they needed to learn more about the game than just the money aspect."

Michael played two seasons and had to finally retire in 2003 due to a chronic knee injury that forced him to do something he had rarely done in his career: sit out games and score in the single digits. He'd only dealt with one significant injury in his career (a broken left foot in 1985) before the tendinitis in his knee weakened his performance considerably. He explained in 2002, before his third and final retirement, "My mind is still consistent, but my body isn't."

That may have been true, but despite all that was holding him back, he still managed to score 40 or more points in eight games as a Wizard. In addition, his shooting average in his first year as a Wizard was among the top 10 in the league. He may not have been as dominant as before, but at 40, Michael could still play better than most players half his age.

LIFE LESSONS FROM HIS AIRNESS

- ● WORK AT YOUR CRAFT AND YOU WILL BE REPAID.
- ● WRITE YOUR OWN STORY.
- ● CREATE NEW CHALLENGES. STAY MOTIVATED.
- ● YOU'RE NEVER TOO OLD TO KEEP TRYING.

STRENGTHEN YOUR BONDS

It's safe to say that if you had Michael on your side, you'd love his fierceness. If you didn't, you'd fear it. Michael knew he needed help to win titles. He needed teammates. He needed coaches and trainers. He needed owners and general managers. He needed a complete, well-rounded team of support. Michael cherished his relationships with most of these people and worked well with all of his coaches, but he was also brutally honest with all of them. He told staff and teammates when they weren't living up to his high standards; he demanded excellence.

Some of his relationships couldn't handle the tough love he offered. Some teammates perceived his slights as a sign of his selfishness in assuming that the whole world revolved around his ideas and opinions. Maybe there was truth to this. Or perhaps it was their jealousy

"I WILL NOT
LET ANYTHING
GET IN THE WAY
OF ME AND
MY COMPETITIVE
ENTHUSIASM
TO WIN."

talking. But it was understood that Michael was willing to push his relationships to the breaking point in order to win.

BE COACHABLE

Michael was always ready to learn. He always wanted to advance his game. Yes, his talent was off the charts, but he knew that there was always room for improvement:

"You can practice shooting eight hours a day, but if your technique is wrong, then all you become is very good at shooting the wrong way. Get the fundamentals down, and the level of everything you do will rise."

On his long road to personal improvement, he built unique working relationships with each of his coaches, all of them founded on respect. Before Michael would listen to someone, he had to hold them in high regard.

By the time he played for coach Dean Smith, the man already had become a legend in Michael's home state of North Carolina. The coach's credibility was there from the start. Michael may have gotten by in high school on his raw talent, but Smith knew it wasn't enough. So he helped educate Michael in the fundamentals. As a result, Coach Smith polished Michael's game in key areas: "Michael wasn't an instant star," he explained, "rather, he was an important part of a potentially great team." About Michael's first year, he said: "The 1982 season was actually an up and down one for him, which is what you'd expect from any freshman. One of the areas that needed work was his outside shot. The problem was that he had such huge hands, which actually made it harder to shoot. It was like trying to shoot a volleyball."

The most critical things Michael learned from Coach Smith were how to play defense and the importance of team basketball. Coach Smith taught Michael about selflessness, a quality Smith exhibited when he let Michael move on to the next step in his basketball journey. He could have advised Michael to stay one more year in college to help UNC win a title, but he didn't. He knew that leaving to play for the NBA was the best decision for Michael and supported him in that choice.

When Michael left North Carolina, having soaked up life and basketball skills from Coach Smith, he was as prepared as he could be. But before he took those lessons to the NBA, he was chosen for the 1984 U.S. Olympic team. The next coach to shape his game would be Bobby Knight, the U.S. Men's Olympic team coach.

Coach Knight was a disciplinarian who had once coached at the United States Military Academy (a.k.a. Army). His no-nonsense approach to basketball—hard workouts and continuous training—meshed well with Michael's hunger to be the best. Knight's coaching style suited Michael's core values. But what didn't work for Michael was Knight's harsh criticism. After one game, Coach Knight was furious at Michael for falling short of expectations: "Mike, when the hell are you going to set a screen?" Knight yelled. "All you're doing is rebounding, passing, and scoring. Dammit, screen somebody out here!"

Though Michael denies this, it was reported that Knight's criticism brought Michael to tears after an Olympic game against Germany in which he had six turnovers.

Despite his harsh words, Knight knew he was coaching a kid with endless talent. He would later rave about his young player's ability: "If I were going to pick people with the best ability I'd ever seen play the game, he'd be one of them. If I wanted to pick the best competitors that I'd ever seen play, he'd be one of them. . . . That, to me, makes him the best basketball player that I've ever seen play."

Overall, Michael didn't love his time with Knight, but under the coach's strict command, he learned to develop a hard shell—something that would serve him well in his professional career. He won the U.S. Olympic gold medal in 1984. He led the team in scoring. That was his coming-out party.

"WINNING HAS A PRICE. AND LEADERSHIP HAS A PRICE."

RAISE THE GAME OF EVERYONE AROUND YOU

When Michael went pro in 1984, he inherited a coach named Kevin Loughery. The year before Michael arrived, Loughery had coached the Bulls to a 27–55 record, missing the playoffs. The team's poor record was what had allowed Chicago to land Michael—they had the third draft pick thanks to their unremarkable standings.

Michael enjoyed a positive working relationship with his new coach. It was clear that Loughery admired Michael's intensity: "Once we started scrimmaging, there was no doubt about his competitiveness," said Loughery, looking back.

He also remembered Michael's teammates struggling with that intensity: "The players weren't happy with Michael in a way because he demanded that they play as hard as he played in every practice and every game. He never took a day off, and in any drill that he was involved in, he wanted to win." It took time for them to see that Michael knew what he was doing and that they could trust him. Loughery watched their relationship evolve: "It's always a test at the beginning for the veteran players to see how good this guy is and what he is all about. But the one thing they didn't realize is that the first day [Michael] walked into camp he became the leader of the team in his mind."

The Bulls made the playoffs that year, thrilling fans and players alike, but the front office wanted more, and they didn't think coach Loughery had more to offer. For that one season, however, Loughery watched a leader and a true competitor bolster his team.

LISTEN TO PEOPLE YOU TRUST

Michael's next coach was Stan Albeck, who coached him for one season (1985–86) after replacing Loughery. Three games into his first season coaching the Bulls, Albeck watched Michael go down with a broken foot. It was a catastrophe. He missed 64 regular-season games. It was torture for Michael not to be on the floor with his teammates. His mental toughness was tested to an extent that it hadn't been before.

STAT ⚡ Over the course of his career, Michael Jordan averaged 31.0 points, 6.3 rebounds, and 5.6 assists in 45 games in Eastern Conference finals.

He came back near the end of the season to help the Bulls get into the playoffs, but Albeck didn't know how to manage Michael's caged energy. Michael didn't want any limitations after returning from his injury. On the other hand, Bulls management wanted to play it safe and monitor his minutes. After all, Michael was their golden goose; they couldn't risk him getting reinjured. Albeck was stuck in the middle, but as Michael later said, Albeck was a coach who always had his back. At the time, Michael's mentality was to play at all cost, so he needed Albeck to save him from himself. He recounts what he said to Bulls owner Jerry Reinsdorf when they were discussing the decision to play through his injury:

"[He said,] 'If you [Michael] had a terrible headache, and I [Reinsdorf] gave you a bottle of pills, and nine of the pills would cure you, and one of the pills would kill you, would you take a pill?' And I look at him, and I said, 'Depends on how [expletive] bad the headache is.'"

In the end, Albeck chose not to jeopardize his star player's career by overplaying him, and Michael had to respect that, despite how painful it was for him to dial back his intensity even a little. Amazingly, Michael played in the first round of the playoffs and scored 63 points in a double-overtime loss to the Boston Celtics on April 20, 1986. It remains an NBA record for most points in a playoff game.

SOME BONDS LAST A LIFETIME

Michael was healthy heading into the 1986–87 season, but he was tired of losing. Coach Stan Albeck had been let go. Michael was about to meet his third head coach in his

THE START OF A WINNING FRIENDSHIP

At the start of their first season together, Michael made Doug Collins a promise. He told Collins that he wouldn't let him lose his first game as an NBA coach. Michael went on to score 50 points and help the Bulls (and his coach) take home the win.

third professional season: Doug Collins, a former NBA All-Star player, Olympian, and broadcaster hired by the Bulls. Collins's resume, which included playing in an NBA final, was enough to gain Michael's trust and give him hope that the Bulls could win.

Even though Collins didn't have Michael's athleticism, he was a former NBA guard, which gave him a better understanding of Michael's position. Michael flourished under Collins and earned his first scoring title. The Bulls, as a team, began to improve, winning 40, 50, and 47 games, respectively, under Collins's three-year stewardship. Collins was instrumental in nurturing the bond between Michael and Scottie Pippen, who developed a partnership that would be rewarded with titles.

The Bulls made it to the Eastern Conference finals in 1989, the first time they'd done so with Michael as part of the team, but they lost to the Detroit Pistons in six games. Collins was fired that summer. Some say Michael had something to do with the Collins firing, but most knew it was a management decision. Michael eventually put the confusion to bed:

> *"It was not Doug Collins's and Michael Jordan's relationship, because he and I were getting closer as we spent more time together. When people say Michael Jordan had something to do with Doug Collins's getting fired, that doesn't have any validity to it."*

Later, when Michael became a part owner of the Washington Wizards

"IT'S ABSOLUTELY WRONG THAT I DON'T WANT GUYS TO CHALLENGE ME. AND THE PEOPLE WHO SAY THAT AREN'T IN THE ROOM."

and president of the Wizards' basketball operations, he hired Doug Collins as his head coach. It was clear that his loyalty to and respect for his old coach remained.

BE OPEN TO NEW STRATEGIES

Some teammate relationships cracked beneath Michael's fierce intensity and pressure. In a famous encounter during practice in the 1995–96 season, Michael got into an altercation with Steve Kerr, a much smaller player. Kerr didn't like the physicality Michael brought to a tough scrimmage, but he didn't back down. Eventually, Michael punched him in the face, leaving Kerr with a black eye. After the altercation, something changed. It took a lot to get Michael's respect, but getting it was crucial to the players on his team.

"I would say it definitely helped our relationship," explained Kerr, referring to the moment he stood up to Michael, "and that probably sounds really weird. I wouldn't recommend that to anybody at home. . . . For me in that case, Michael was definitely testing me,

and I responded. I feel like I kind of passed the test, and he trusted me more afterward."

Michael couldn't stand players who didn't work hard. But he accepted those who stood up to him—as long as they did it in the right way.

Michael eventually apologized to Kerr and their relationship improved. But, even after being punched in the face by Michael, Kerr couldn't deny that his teammate knew what he was doing: "What made him a badass was that he wasn't just a talent," Kerr said. "It was the understanding of it all, the work ethic, the game itself, the strategy involved. He got it all; he understood all of it. He was absolutely one of the smartest players I've ever played with."

The one person who managed all this tension was Phil Jackson, Michael's newest head coach. Jackson had been promoted from assistant coach to head coach after Collins was fired in 1989. Jackson was known as the "Zen Master" because of his calming, intellectual approach to the game. He would give players books to read that preached motivation, calmness, and relaxation. His Buddhist mantras became legendary, and Michael listened and learned:

> *"No matter how much pressure there is in a game, I think to myself: It's still just a game. I don't meditate, but I know what he's [Jackson's] getting at. He's teaching about peacefulness and living in the moment, but not losing the aggressive attitude. Not being reckless, but strategic. What I do is challenge myself in big games. . . . I don't want to rush. . . . These are things Phil has taught me. And I'll tell you, it all works."*

While Jackson taught inner peace and calm, he was also well versed in the physical game. He was considered a defensive stalwart on the Knicks when they won the title in 1973. This past victory gave him cachet in the locker room—he was a winner. Jackson knew that his accomplishments in basketball mattered to players like Michael.

At first, Michael didn't quite like the triangle offense that assistant coach Tex Winters taught and Coach Jackson quickly adopted. The triangle created good spacing between players and allowed each one to pass to four teammates. The offense would no longer need to go through Michael all the time, so Michael had to come to terms with that. Thankfully, Michael was off-the-charts brilliant and willing to adapt. Soon there would be nothing stopping the Bulls.

Once Michael adjusted to the new offensive strategy, the outcome was everything Jackson hoped it would be. The Bulls won games using their triangle offense and got closer to securing titles. In the end, they earned six titles in Jackson's nine seasons coaching the Bulls.

KNOW YOUR LIMITS

Jackson was the glue that held the Bulls together. He managed the competing egos of Rodman, Pippen, and even Michael. Michael saw what Jackson had accomplished and understood that being a great coach wasn't easy. When he retired from basketball the final time, many people asked him if he would pursue coaching. He had

"I TRY TO FIND A QUIET CENTER WITHIN ME BECAUSE THERE'S SO MUCH HYPE OUT THERE, AND I DON'T WANT TO FALL INTO IT."

watched Magic Johnson try his hand at coaching. He'd seen plenty of other all-time greats give it a shot. Some, like Larry Bird, had success, but others struggled with the limits of inferior players. It was just too frustrating for them. Michael knew his limitations and didn't kid himself:

"I don't think I would have the patience for [coaching]. So in essence, coaching is something that I've never really felt I could do from an emotional standpoint because . . . I have a different perspective about things than what the kids do today."

Where others might try to force it, Michael had been through enough coaches to realize that it wasn't for him. Michael just didn't see himself storming the sidelines in a suit and tie, waving his hands, and shouting instructions to players on the court. Coaching didn't have the same level of control over the game that he was used to as a player. He belonged in No. 23, wearing sneakers on his feet and holding a ball in his hands—that's where he had all the power he needed.

LIFE LESSONS FROM HIS AIRNESS

- ● DON'T APOLOGIZE FOR RAISING THE STANDARD.
- ● RESPECT IS MORE IMPORTANT THAN FRIENDSHIP.
- ● LISTEN, LEARN, AND BE COACHABLE.
- ● TRY NEW STRATEGIES ON THE ROAD TO SUCCESS.
- ● WINNING TEAMS ARE BUILT ON TRUST.

PLAY IT FORWARD

CHAPTER 8

We live in a society that's focused on the freshest new talent and the latest trends. We have no time for the past. We sometimes forget about the trailblazers, but history teaches us to look back because there was always someone there before us—someone who laid the groundwork for future generations. Michael never forgot the trailblazers. He understood and appreciated that there were players who paved the way for his success, including Jerry West and Julius "Dr. J" Erving:

"In the 1950s and 1960s, you have Joe DiMaggio and Jackie Robinson. But Julius Erving was the first basketball player to combine dramatic athletic ability on the court with a clean, positive image off the court that connected with corporate America."

As a kid, he knew more about Dr. J. than any other player. Later, he was inspired by Erving's commercial deals with Coca-Cola. It would give him the confidence to work his own deals with Nike.

"WHEN I CAME INTO THE LEAGUE, I WASN'T NEARLY AS ENAMORED WITH MAGIC JOHNSON AND LARRY BIRD AS I WAS WITH JULIUS ERVING."

Michael also respected another trailblazer who preceded Dr. J's 1970s and early 1980s career: Jerry West, a slick guard who played for the Lakers from 1960–73 and brought home a title. West was so smooth and revered (a.k.a. "Mr. Clutch") that the NBA made his silhouette their logo—the same logo used today. Once Michael became established in the league, many thought his silhouette should replace West's. Michael didn't endorse that change. He had too much respect for West and the legacy he'd left behind.

Not surprisingly, the respect went both ways. West was a big fan of Michael:

"I'm not sure we've seen a player like him in my lifetime," he said of the talent that came after him. "Because of his impressive play on both ends of the court," West continued, "he was arguably, well I don't think arguably, he was the best offensive player and the best defensive player in the league; we haven't seen that. But the competitive nature of Michael was just unique."

ALWAYS BE (KIND OF) HUMBLE
Michael rarely backs down, but he does know his place in history. When people ask him if he is the greatest of all time, he pays respect to the legends instead of soaking up all

the praise. He explains why he can't claim the title of GOAT:

"I didn't play against all the great players prior to me, and I had those other players to influence my game. It's a great honor, don't get me wrong, but I would've loved to play against Jerry West to determine if I was a better guard than him or Oscar Robertson. But we'll never know."

Michael always wanted to test himself against the best players, the ones who came before and after him. There's no argument that he was able to be the best while he was playing. He had the scoring stats, NBA titles, and other accolades to back him. But he believed that you couldn't draw a fair comparison between one era of basketball and another:

"There is no such thing as a perfect basketball player, and I don't believe there is only one greatest player either. Everyone plays in different eras. I built my talents on the shoulders of someone else's talent. I believe greatness is an evolutionary process that changes and evolves from era to era."

IMITATION IS THE SINCEREST FORM OF FLATTERY

Michael's unique combination of flair, power, finesse, and craft had never been seen before— especially from a shooting guard. He was revered by fans the world over, particularly the young ones.

Kids would simulate his moves on playgrounds. They would try a duck-and-under move, a fadeaway jump shot from the baseline, and maybe even attempt one of his showstopping dunks. But there was one kid watching Michael closer than anyone: Kobe Bryant, who was just six years old when Michael went pro.

Michael and Kobe's careers only briefly overlapped. Kobe was drafted in 1996; Michael retired for the last time in 2003. They played against each other only eight times in the regular season, as Kobe was just starting and Michael was finishing up his career.

Though they belonged to different basketball eras, their similarities were hard to ignore. Both were six-foot-six shooting guards with lethal jump shots, sky-high vertical leaps, and dunks that were out of this world. But the most notable

"WITHOUT JULIUS ERVING, DAVID THOMPSON, WALTER DAVIS, AND ELGIN BAYLOR, THERE WOULD NEVER HAVE BEEN A MICHAEL JORDAN. I EVOLVED FROM THEM."

"SOME PEOPLE WANT IT TO HAPPEN, SOME WISH IT WOULD HAPPEN, OTHERS MAKE IT HAPPEN."

similarity between them was their competitive nature. Some say Kobe may have been even fiercer, something Michael would likely dispute. After all, Michael had won six titles, and Kobe had won five. They both had a will to win that drove them harder than anyone else. They both were hard on teammates (for Kobe, it was Shaq who took the heat). Everyone knew that Kobe looked up to Michael and copied many of his styles. But Kobe wanted to be his own man too, saying, "I don't want to be the next Michael Jordan. I only want to be Kobe Bryant."

In turn, Michael saw something special in the up-and-coming player. So, after the Bulls beat the Lakers in December 1997, he couldn't help but give the 18-year-old a nod, telling reporters, "I think it's just a matter of time for him. You realize how good he is."

Toward the end of his career, Kobe explained why it didn't concern him who was better or who would win in a one-on-one: "I feel like, yo, what you get from me is from him. I don't get five championships here without him because he guided me so much and gave me so much great advice."

Kobe added: "It was a rough couple of years for me coming into the league. . . . And at that point, Michael provided a lot of guidance for me. Like, I had a question about shooting his turnaround shot, so I asked him about it. And he gave me a great, detailed answer. But on top of that, he said, 'If you ever need anything, give me a call.'"

Michael had a generous and giving side. He understood what Kobe was going through: The hype. The media attention. Coming out of high school right into the pros. Kobe was being dubbed "the next Jordan." Michael saw himself in Kobe's struggle to perform under all that pressure.

Kobe's tragic death in 2020 hit Michael hard. Michael could be stoic and fierce on the court, but his soft side was there under the hard exterior. At Kobe's memorial service, he did his best to express how he felt: "Everyone

"KOBE WAS MY DEAR FRIEND. HE WAS LIKE A LITTLE BROTHER."

always wanted to talk about the comparisons between him and me. I just wanted to talk about Kobe." He finished his speech with, "I will live with the memories of knowing that I had a little brother and I tried to help in every way I could. Please, rest in peace little brother."

BE INCOMPARABLE; GUARD YOUR LEGACY

While he was still playing, Michael was aware of young players being compared to him, and he did not appreciate it. His off-the-scale competitiveness did not allow room for other players to even be considered in his zip code of talent. He firmly believed that nobody

could outwork him. It wasn't until after he retired that he gave a few young players some (but not all) of the kudos they deserved.

When he first entered the league, Michael himself had been compared to Julius Erving and Oscar Robertson. It was a lot to live up to. When Michael retired for the last time, LeBron James was just entering the NBA straight out of high school, so naturally, the comparisons started.

LeBron gave Michael all the praise. He'd watched Michael growing up and emulated him. Unfortunately, Michael didn't reciprocate the praise; he was tough on LeBron:

"HEART IS WHAT SEPARATES THE GOOD FROM THE GREAT."

"Is he capable? Yes. He has the skills that most 18-year-olds do not have. Now, if you equate that to playing in the league, I think he would be an average player in our league right now with the potential to be a better player. To say that he can step in at the same level as a Tracy McGrady or a Kobe Bryant would be unfair to LeBron James."

Michael, always the competitor, wouldn't give LeBron too much too soon.

LeBron never saw Michael's comments as a slight. When he was a teenager and first met Michael, he was awestruck: "It was godly. I've said that over and over before, but it was like meeting God for the first time. That's what I felt like as a 16-year-old kid when I met MJ."

Once LeBron played in the league and won championships, Michael softened his stance on him, probably because he knew he would never have to face him.

Michael's mantra is never to show weakness. He never wanted to reveal to an opponent how they could get the upper hand. If he were sick, he would hide it. If he had an injury, he would play harder to cover it up. Giving LeBron praise would weaken his stature. Michael didn't know how to pass the torch. But he also knew that LeBron's talents couldn't be overlooked.

Michael understood that many people wanted to "Be Like Mike." Kobe, LeBron, and countless others had come up trying to accomplish what he had worked so hard to achieve. It wasn't always easy to be a role model to so many players who were trying to push him off the Mount Rushmore of basketball players.

AVOID THE PITFALLS OF FAME

At the height of his fame and in the years that followed, Michael couldn't go anywhere without being mobbed. When he was on the Olympic "Dream Team" in 1992, he was surrounded by people as he walked the streets of Barcelona. In

Asia, he was swarmed. There was nothing normal about his life.

When the Bulls were winning championships throughout the 1990s, Michael would have to hide in his hotel room before games. It was only natural that he found his escape doing what he loved:

> *"On the basketball court, I worry about nothing. When I'm out there, no one can bother me. . . . I don't have to think about anything. If I have a problem off the court, I find that after I play, my mind is clearer and I can come up with a better solution. It's like therapy. It relaxes me and allows me to solve problems."*

Throughout Michael's career, the spotlight on him was more intense than the sun, but at times it dimmed just enough for him to breathe a little easier. Whether he liked it or not, Michael was an international celebrity, so he had to learn how to manage the expectations of teammates, fans, coaches, and the media.

Michael dealt with the scrutiny and fame by becoming a master of self-preservation. He surrounded himself with a small yet mighty inner circle of people he could trust. His main support system was led by Ahmad Rashad, a former NFL player who turned into a well-known sideline reporter for NBC's basketball coverage. He met Michael in 1990 in Los Angeles at Magic Johnson's "Midsummer Night's Classic," a charity event. They exchanged numbers and have been friends and confidants ever since.

Aside from Rashad, Michael distrusted the media after getting burned one too many times, most notably by *Sports Illustrated,* which criticized him with the cover headline, "Bag It, Michael!: Jordan and the White Sox Are Embarrassing Baseball." Michael never gave *SI* an interview again.

Michael is fiercely loyal to the people who are loyal to him. He has close celebrity friends who understand the pitfalls of fame and can identify

EXPECT LOYALTY

Michael Jordan's best friend throughout the 1980s, 1990s, and 2000s was Charles Barkley. They played golf together. They were on the 1992 Olympic "Dream Team" together. They teased each other brutally as only best friends could.

But Michael's friendship can be a tentative thing. All Barkley had to do was question him on air, saying, "I don't know if Michael's ever going to be successful [running the Charlotte Hornets] because I don't know if he got enough strong people around him." Michael has not talked to Barkley since.

with the problems it brings. But Michael will also befriend the most unlikely of people—his best friend is a limo driver he met in 1984. On the flip side, if he feels that you have betrayed him, the way he felt that *Sports Illustrated* had, then he is done with you.

This attitude may seem cold and lonely, but it was necessary for Michael—on and off the court. He

"THE BASKETBALL COURT FOR ME, DURING A GAME, IS THE MOST PEACEFUL PLACE I CAN IMAGINE."

had to protect his time and energy. He had to put a shield around himself to block the daggers. It's what allowed him to perform at an elite level. "My fame is, it was good in the beginning," Michael said. "Anytime people talking about you in a positive way, yeah, it's great to hear those comments."

He also knew there was a price to pay for fame:

"Now that you're on a pedestal, it's not just the positive talking that you're hearing. You hear some points and some people taking shots at you and that really changes the whole idea of being out there for people to see you."

LIFE LESSONS FROM HIS AIRNESS

- HONOR THOSE WHO PAVED THE WAY FOR YOU.
- DON'T COMPARE YOURSELF TO OTHERS. MAKE YOUR OWN MARK.
- SUPPORT THOSE WHO FOLLOW IN YOUR FOOTSTEPS, EVEN IF THAT MEANS SHOWING TOUGH LOVE.
- LEAVE YOUR HATERS IN THE DUST.
- CHOOSE YOUR FRIENDS CAREFULLY.

OPEN NEW DOORS

CHAPTER 9

After they retire, elite athletes face the same dilemma: what to do next. For most of their professional lives, they are ruled by a schedule. They practice, play games, rest, run, lift weights. They have a locker room where they can socialize. They travel. They get exorbitant amounts of attention. That structure, activity, and attention all go away when they retire.

Michael was so dedicated to the game, so regimented, and so accustomed to the spotlight, that many worried he'd be miserable postretirement.

Lucky for Michael, the spotlight stayed with him when he retired for good in 2003 at age 40. He kept himself busy doing commercials, working on his Jordan Brand,

playing golf, helping charities, and spending time with family.

Michael was always looking for the next challenge, even as he entered retirement. He knew only one speed: to train to be a champion. Finally, after a few years, he settled on a worthy challenge, something that would drive him in that same

"I'VE NEVER BEEN AFRAID TO FAIL."

way. He decided to return home and take ownership of a team. It was time to go back to where it all started: North Carolina.

OWN YOUR CHOICES

It was only natural for Michael to find his way back to the state where he grew up and played for the University of North Carolina. It was 2006, just three years after his retirement when Michael purchased a minor stake in the Charlotte Bobcats, a team that later became the Charlotte Hornets. Eventually, he bought the team for $275 million, making him the league's only African American majority owner.

The Hornets haven't enjoyed nearly as much success as everyone expected. In fact, in 2012, their win-loss record was the worst in NBA history. From there, the team acquired Kemba Walker and, with him, a little more respect, but the Hornets haven't managed to advance past the first round of playoffs since Michael took the helm. For a man accustomed to winning, it can't be easy to watch his team falter. But true to Michael's personality, he shows no signs of giving up. Losing just makes him want to win more. During one tough spell for the Hornets, he expressed his deep sense of responsibility to his team's success. He never wanted to be seen as a failure, but he wasn't too proud to admit that even he could fail:

"Ultimately if you can say that I'm a bad owner and we're winning championships, I can live with that. But if we're not

making the playoffs and we're spending and losing money, then I have to look in the mirror and say I'm not taking the necessary steps to do what it takes to run an organization."

As he had during his playing years, Michael understood that if he didn't produce a win, he would have to take the hit. Never one to duck out of his responsibility, he was ready and willing to absorb the blame. The buck stopped with him. In some ways, that kind of risk made the whole experience more interesting for him.

STAY SHARP

Michael has been honing his golf game since college. In retirement, golf helped to fill the competitive void left by basketball. Never one to show moderation, Michael is a member of 12 private golf clubs and owns more than 40 golf club sets. He even decked out his home with a 3,500-square-foot putting green for everyday practice.

Michael is just as ruthless on the golf course as he was on the court. There are plenty of high-stake games against well-known opponents, including ex-teammates, pro golfers like Tiger Woods and Rickie Fowler, and former president Bill Clinton. He plays against anyone he thinks will give him a good battle and provide the competitive rush he craves:

"For a competitive junkie like me, golf is a great solution because it smacks you in the face every time you think you have accomplished something. That to me has taken over a lot of the energy and competitiveness for basketball."

He tries to keep his golf game casual, but his nature doesn't allow for too much of that. Instead, he wagers on holes and trash-talks like he is still on the court.

HOLD THE DOOR OPEN

Once his playing days were over, Michael had the time and focus to give back to his community. Even the messaging in his Nike and Jordan brand ads became more thoughtful and inclusive. For example, in a series of commercials

MAKE IT WORTH YOUR WHILE

Forbes valued the Hornets at about $1.6 billion in 2021, a sizeable increase from when Michael Jordan secured his majority ownership with $275 million in 2006. While the team hasn't earned him a championship ring, it has helped make Michael the fifth-richest African American today.

he made with the "Become Legendary" theme, he gave credit to the unknowns trying to make it in a difficult world. With images of star athletes interspersed with regular kids trying to make their way, we hear what sounds like Michael's inner monologue:

"I know what is within me, even if you can't see it yet. Look me in the eyes. I have something more important than courage. I have patience. I will become what I know I am."

In the old "Be Like Mike" ads, he portrayed an image of what others thought of him. In these new ads, he portrayed what *he* wanted people to see: more of his truth. He wanted his story to inspire others and give them the resolve to follow their dreams.

Michael's pay-it-forward attitude is evident in how he shares his money with those less fortunate. His relationship with the Make-A-Wish foundation has lasted over 30 years. He became an ambassador for the program in 2008 and has donated more than $5 million to the nonprofit over the years. He also hosts an annual golf expo that encourages other celebrities to pay it forward. From 2001 to 2014, Michael gathered his celebrity friends, including Wayne Gretzky, Chevy Chase, Samuel L. Jackson, and Mark Wahlberg for the annual Michael Jordan Celebrity Invitational. Invitees choose their favorite charities and donate their winnings. Michael's proceeds from this event have been donated to Cats Care, the James R. Jordan Foundation, Keep Memory Alive, and Opportunity Village.

STILL SETTING RECORDS

In 2014, Michael became the first billionaire player in **NBA** history. His current net worth is now close to $1.6 billion.

In 2016, he gave $5 million to become a founding donor of the Smithsonian's National Museum of African American History and Culture. He also gave $10 million in 2021 to open two new medical clinics in his hometown of Wilmington, North Carolina, to help uninsured and underinsured residents get the treatment they need.

BE THE BEST FATHER YOU CAN BE

Michael met his first wife, Juanita Vanoy, early on in his career. They were married in 1989 and had three children together: two sons, Jeffrey and Marcus, and a daughter named Jasmine. His marriage ended in 2006, just a few years after he retired. He married Yvette Prieto seven years later and had two more children: Ysabel and Victoria. Like any father, it was important to Michael to be there for all his kids. He aimed to be the kind of parent his father was:

"My father, he was there when I didn't understand. He was there when I was wrong. He was there when I cried. He was there when I lied. For some reason, my dad was always there when I needed him most. His love was never-ending."

He raised his kids to love sports but hoped they wouldn't feel too hindered by the extra pressure of his celebrity. He understood that his kids would be held to a higher standard as athletes just because they were his. Jeffrey and Marcus played on the same team together in high school and led the team to the best season in Loyola Academy's history. From there, they both went on to play in college. Michael offered this advice when it became clear that his oldest wanted to make a name for himself just like his father had:

"The thing that we have tried to tell Jeff is that you set your own

"THE GAME IS MY WIFE. IT DEMANDS LOYALTY AND RESPONSIBILITY, AND IT GIVES ME BACK FULFILLMENT AND PEACE."

expectations. By no means in this world can you ever live up to someone else's expectations of who you are."

Jeffrey and Marcus may not have gone on to play in the NBA, but all three of Michael's grown children have worked for Nike's Jordan brand and, at some point, found their place in the world of sports and entertainment. "They wanted to be like their dad," their mom, Juanita, said back in 2013. What kid wouldn't?

LIFE LESSONS FROM HIS AIRNESS

- GO BACK TO YOUR ROOTS.
- FIND A HOBBY AND EXCEL AT IT.
- BE SELFLESS AND GIVE BACK.
- SHARE YOUR PASSION WITH OTHERS.

LEAVE A LEGACY

CHAPTER 10

With so much time having passed since his playing days, Michael can reflect more easily on his experiences. He has immense gratitude for what he was able to accomplish and for the great fortune he's had since he was that skinny five-foot-ten-inch kid from Wilmington, North Carolina, who wanted to be on UNC's varsity team. That kid emerged into a powerhouse athlete who would take the world of basketball by storm.

Even Michael, who had set his goals higher than just about everyone else, could now finally sit back and be satisfied and thankful knowing that he had reached them.

BE IRREPLACEABLE

In 1996, during the NBA's 50th anniversary season, an elite team of experts and athletes decided to come up with the 50 Greatest Players in NBA History. Media, former players, coaches, and current team executives voted to see who would be on that list. The final list wasn't

"PEOPLE ASK ME IF I COULD FLY, I SAID, 'YEAH . . . FOR A LITTLE WHILE.'"

ranked, and was made up of a group of players who had achieved a total of 107 titles and more than 400 NBA All-Star Game selections, and had earned nearly one million points.

It was a list that included Wilt Chamberlain, Julius Erving, Jerry West, and Shaquille O'Neal. It did not surprise anyone that Michael Jordan made the list. Today, someone might question whether players like Kobe Bryant, LeBron James, and many others who came up after 1996 could knock some of the older players off this list. But no one is wondering if Michael will be replaced. No matter the era, Michael will forever remain one of the greatest players of all time.

AIM TO INSPIRE

Michael's incredible career is an aspirational tale that parents and coaches alike can share with children about the long, arduous path to becoming a championship competitor. The next generation and the one after that will take notice of Michael's relentless determination to win. Not just on the basketball court but in other facets of his life. Knowing he put in that kind of effort makes him wholly at peace with his accomplishments. Trying; striving to be better, was all he ever did. And he's not done yet.

"EVEN WHEN
I'M OLD AND GRAY,
I WON'T BE ABLE
TO PLAY IT,
BUT I'LL STILL
LOVE THE GAME."

"I WANT TO BE THE BRIDGE TO THE NEXT GENERATION."

PARTING WORDS

The final chapter of Michael's playing days took place on a stage in 2009 as he was inducted into the Basketball Hall of Fame. This holiest of grail's honor is the icing on the cake of any NBA career. It's the final validation. In a 23-minute speech, Michael let it all out. He thanked people. He told stories. He talked about his family and coaches. He even unleashed his feelings about more than a few grudges, some dating back to his high school days. But his speech made an impact because it encompassed everything he is as a player and a person: unapologetically talented and happy to exceed the limits placed on him. Whether he's giving a speech to millions or soaring through the air in his signature No. 23, Michael Jordan never fails to wow an audience and he always brings the fans to their feet.

LIFE LESSONS FROM HIS AIRNESS

- LEAVE A LEGACY YOU'RE PROUD OF.
- INSPIRE OTHERS TO DREAM.
- BE GRATEFUL FOR ALL OF IT.

"I NEVER TOOK A SHORTCUT, AND I NEVER WANTED ANYONE ELSE TO TAKE A SHORTCUT. IF THAT MEANT SOMEONE INTERPRETED ME AS A TYRANT, I'M PRETTY SURE THEY'RE APPRECIATIVE NOW."

IMAGINE WHAT THEY'LL SAY

The true measure of a person is what people say and think about you, and how you are remembered. Michael changed the game and people's lives forever, and you hear that in the way his coaches, teammates, sportscasters, and fellow legends talk about him:

Will McDonough, legendary sportswriter: *"Overall, I think Michael Jordan is the greatest athlete in any particular sport. He dominated the game for the Chicago Bulls and brought the NBA to its greatest peak of popularity."*

Phil Knight, Nike chairman emeritus: *"You can't explain much in 60 seconds, but when you show Michael Jordan, you don't have to. It's that simple."*

Magic Johnson, LA Laker Hall of Famer: *"Once Michael gets up there he says, 'Well, maybe I'll just hang up here in the air for a while, just sit back.' Then all of a sudden, he says, 'Well, maybe I'll 360. No, I changed my mind. I'll go up on the other side.' He's just incredible."*

Larry Bird, Boston Celtic Hall of Famer: *"I think he's God disguised as Michael Jordan."*

Dwyane Wade, three-time NBA champion: *"I come from a Jordan era. I am biased and I'm going to be biased until the day I pass away. Michael Jordan will be my GOAT."*

Phil Jackson, 13-time NBA champion player and coach: *"He didn't miss games. He played hurt, with pain, when he was sick. He came out and performed at an intense level. I don't think anybody ever went away disappointed after watching Michael."*

Elgin Baylor, NBA legend and Hall of Famer: *"If you look up the definition of greatness in the dictionary, it will say Michael Jordan."*

Dani Alves, Barcelona soccer legend: *"I think we always look up to legends and people who not only win but give us a larger-than-life role model. . . . I think Michael Jordan is this, someone who became bigger than his sport."*

B. J. Armstrong, Chicago Bulls teammate: *"To me, [this is] the brilliance of Michael Jordan. He was an incredible, amazing individual player who matched his talents to the team, matched the team's talents to him, and he lived in the middle of those extremes. I don't know how you do that."*

THIS IS NOT THE END

The game of basketball has been everything to me. My refuge. My place I've always gone when I needed to find comfort and peace. It's been a source of intense pain, and a source of [the] most intense feelings of joy and satisfaction. And one that no one can even imagine. It's been a relationship that has evolved over time, and given me the greatest respect and love for the game. It has provided me with a platform to share my passion with millions in a way I neither expected nor could have imagined in my career. I hope that it's given the millions of people that I've touched the optimism and the desire to achieve their goals through hard work, perseverance, and positive attitude. Although I'm recognized with this tremendous honor of being in the basketball Hall of Fame—I don't look at this moment as a defining end to my relationship with the game of basketball. It's simply a continuation of something that I started a long time ago.

—MICHAEL JORDAN,
Hall of Fame induction
speech, September 11, 2009

RESOURCES

MAGAZINES/ NEWSPAPER/WEBSITES

"All the Way Up"
SLAM, June 24, 2016

"Dream Team Debut Was a Rout
of Epic Proportions"
ESPN.com, July 26, 2017

"How Air Jordan Became
Crying Jordan"
The New Yorker, May 11, 2016

"How Michael Jordan
Became Great"
CNBC.com, April 21, 2020

"How Michael Jordan, Magic
Johnson and Larry Bird Led the
Dream Team to Olympic Gold"
biography.com, April 20, 2020

"How Michael Jordan
Re-Defined His Game to
Extend Legendary Career"
bleacherreport.com,
August 21, 2013

"Michael Jordan: A History
of Flight"
ESPN.com, May 19, 2020

"Michael Jordan at 50: Twenty-
Three Impressive Stats from No. 23"
sportingnews.com,
February 15, 2013

"Michael Jordan Becomes Majority
Owner of Charlotte Bobcats"
bleacherreport.com,
March 18, 2010

Michael Jordan Biography
biography.com, April 29, 2014

"Michael Jordan Didn't Make
Varsity—At First"
Newsweek, October 17, 2015

"Michael Jordan: 'I Can No Longer Stay Silent'"
theundefeated.com, July 25, 2016

"Michael Jordan: Icon"
GQ, May 15, 2020

"Michael Jordan on Dean Smith"
The Washington Post,
February 8, 2015

"Michael Jordan Shockingly Names Only Player He 'Couldn't Do Anything' About"
International Business Times,
April 21, 2021

Michael Jordan stats
basketball-reference.com

"Michael Jordan's Iconic Turnaround Fadeaway Jump Shot—How'd He Do That?"
skysports.com, May 18, 2020

"Michael Jordan's Superpower, the Legacy of His Father"
Sports Illustrated, May 10, 2020

"Michael Jordan's Unofficial Guide to Success in the NBA"
bleacherreport.com,
February 14, 2013

NBA 75th Anniversary Team Player Profile: Michael Jordan
nba.com, accessed:
December 7, 2021

"NBA Star Julius Erving Turns 70 Today: Where Is 'Dr. J' Now?"
sportscasting.com,
February 22, 2020

"Pro Basketball; The Final Word from Michael Jordan"
The New York Times,
January 14, 1999

U.S. Men's Olympic Games Records
usab.com, October 21, 2021

"Why Michael Jordan's Return with the Wizards Was More Impressive Than You Think"
sportingnews.com,
September 25, 2021

"I WANT TO BE PERCEIVED AS A GUY WHO PLAYED HIS BEST IN ALL FACETS, NOT JUST SCORING. A GUY WHO LOVED CHALLENGES."

BOOKS

The Jordan Rules: The Inside Story of One Turbulent Season with Michael Jordan and the Chicago Bulls, Sam Smith

The Magic of Teamwork: Proven Principles for Building a Winning Team, Pat Williams

Michael Jordan: The Life, Roland Lazenby

Playing for Keeps: Michael Jordan and the World He Made, David Halberstam

Relentless: From Good to Great to Unstoppable, Tim S. Grover

INTERVIEWS/SPEECHES

"Kobe Bryant Memorial Service"
https://www.latimes.com/california/story/2020-02-24/how-to-watch-kobe-bryant-memorial
February 24, 2020
Staples Center,
Los Angeles, California

"The Last Dance" Documentary
ESPN, 2020

"Michael Jordan's Hall of Fame Speech"
https://www.youtube.com/watch?v=XLzBMGXfK4c
September 11, 2009
Naismith Memorial Basketball Hall of Fame,
Springfield, Massachusetts

"One-on-One with Michael Jordan"
Cigar Aficionado, July/August 2005